D1148779

Pascal
Made Simple

Made Simple *Programming Series*

● **easy to follow** ● **jargon free** ● **task based** ● **practical exercises**

Thousands of people have already discovered that the **MADE SIMPLE** computer applications books give them what they want *fast!* Now, using the same tried, tested and successful formula, Butterworth Heinemann brings you a **new** MADE SIMPLE series focusing on programming languages.

The MADE SIMPLE programming books are easy to follow, jargon free, task based, clear, well presented, and excellent value for money. They also have the **added value of exercises** at the end of each section, **with answers** at the end of the book, to help you in self study as well as in class study. These books follow the maxim: *you learn by doing*.

Unlike most others, the MADE SIMPLE programming books do not get you bogged down in theory, but **give you the essentials fast** and **start you programming right away**, testing you as you go along. Through their clear and concise explanations – and many examples – you will soon understand the key words, techniques, procedures and functions, and start **programming with confidence**.

The MADE SIMPLE Programming Books are in your local bookshop now, or in case of difficulty, direct from:

Heinemann Publishers, Oxford, P.O.Box 381, Oxford, OX2 8EJ.
Tel: 01865 314300. Fax 01865 314091, Credit Card Sales 01865 314627

PROGRAMMING SERIES TITLES:

C	Conor Sexton	0 7506 3244 5	
C++	Conor Sexton	0 7506 3243 7	
Delphi	Stephen Morris	0 7506 3246 1	
Visual Basic	Stephen Morris	0 7506 3245 3	
Pascal	P.K. McBride	0 7506 3242 9	
Java	P.K. McBride	0 7506 3241 0	Summer '97
Visual C++	Stephen Morris	0 7506 3570 3	Summer '97
Windows 95 Programming	Stephen Morris	0 7506 3572 X	Summer '97
Unix	P.K. McBride	0 7506 3571 1	Summer '97

Visit us on the World Wide Web:

http://www.bh.com

Pascal
Made Simple

P.K. McBride

MADE SIMPLE
BOOKS

ID No: 97003104

Dewey No:

Date Acq:

Made Simple
An imprint of Butterworth-Heinemann
Linacre House, Jordan Hill, Oxford OX2 8DP
A division of Reed Educational and Professional Publishing Ltd

   A member of the Reed Elsevier plc group

OXFORD   BOSTON   JOHANNESBURG
MELBOURNE   NEW DELHI   SINGAPORE

First published 1997
©P.K. McBride 1997

All rights reserved. No part of this publication
may be reproduced in any material form (including
photocopying or storing in any medium by electronic
means and whether or not transiently or incidentally
to some other use of this publication) without the
written permission of the copyright holder except in
accordance with the provisions of the Copyright,
Design and Patents Act 1988 or under the terms of a
licence issued by the Copyright Licensing Agency Ltd,
90 Tottenham Court Road, London, England W1P 9HE.
Applications for the copyright holder's written permission
to reproduce any part of this publication should be addressed
to the publishers

TRADEMARKS/REGISTERED TRADEMARKS
Computer hardware and software brand names mentioned in this book are protected
by their respective trademarks and are acknowledged.

British Library Cataloguing in Publication Data
A catalogue record for this book is available from the British Library

ISBN 0 7506 3242 9

Typeset by P.K.McBride, Southampton

Archtype, Bash Casual, Cotswold and Gravity fonts from Advanced Graphics Ltd
Icons designed by Sarah Ward © 1994
Printed and bound in Great Britain by Scotprint, Musselburgh, Scotland

Contents

Preface

Pascal has become well established as a language for students. It is one of the easiest to learn, lends itself naturally to a structured approach to programming and produces clear and readable code. Though it is little used for the production of commercial software, it provides an excellent base for learning other languages. C and C++, for example, are the languages of choice for applications, operating systems, games and other programs where speed is needed. Both are difficult to learn as a first language, but do not prove half so impenetrable if you have cut your programming teeth on Pascal. Borland's Delphi, which is currently finding favour with developers of databases and other commercial applications, is another language that would be easier to learn if you already have a grasp of Pascal.

This book does not attempt to give a complete coverage of the language. The aim is to provide clear and concise explanations – with plenty of simple examples – of the words that create the program structures, and of the key procedures and functions.

For most of the book, the focus is on that central core of Pascal that is common to all versions of the language. The techniques and programs given in the first seven chapters should work on any computer, from PC to multi-user system, that has a Pascal compiler. Chapter 8 gives an introduction to Turbo Pascal, in its Windows version, and Turbo appears again in the summary of the language in Chapter 10.

You can only learn programming by doing it. With this in mind, there are exercises at the end of each of the first seven chapters, with answers in Chapter 9.

1 Pascal essentials

What is Pascal?

The Pascal programming language was developed, around 20 years ago, by Nicholas Wirth. It was designed as a first language for programming students, and serves that purpose well. Pascal is one of the easiest languages to learn, and it encourages beginners to develop good programming habits.

It is easy to learn mainly because the language has a relatively small set of words, and these are close enough to ordinary English to be easy to understand and remember. Even before you start to learn the language, you should be able to read a Pascal program's code and be able to make some sense of it, For example, here is a Pascal version of the "Hello World" program – a classic first program in many language tutorials.

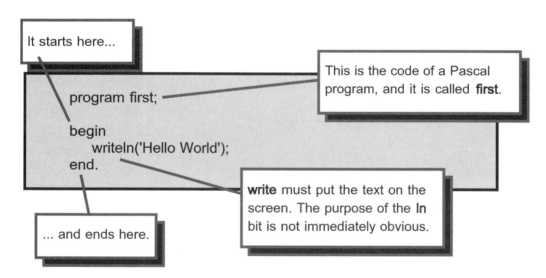

It starts here...

This is the code of a Pascal program, and it is called **first**.

```
program first;

begin
     writeln('Hello World');
end.
```

... and ends here.

write must put the text on the screen. The purpose of the **ln** bit is not immediately obvious.

It encourages good programming habits because it is a *structured* language. Programs written in Pascal fall naturally into blocks, each handling a distinct operation. Not only is the resulting code easier to read and debug, but you may be able to reuse some of those blocks – in the same program or possibly in later ones – where you want to perform the same operations.

2

Program and program code

The process of creating a Pascal program starts in a text editor. Here you write the *program code*, saving it as a file with a **.PAS** extension. Computers cannot understand Pascal text – the language is meant for human consumption. Before you can run a Pascal program on a computer, the text must be turned into *machine language*. This is done through a *compiler*.

The compiler works in two stages. The first stage is to check the code for syntax errors – mis-spelled or mis-used commands, punctuation mistakes, or items out of sequence. If the compiler finds any errors, it will report them and stop work. The programmer must then take the code back into an editor and debug it – remove the errors. The code is passed to the compiler again – and may well be thrown back for further debugging. When all the errors have been cleared, the compiler will move on to the second stage and turn the code into an executable program.

Type in this simple example, and save it as *first.pas*. If you are using Turbo Pascal on a PC, the **Compile** command will compile into a file called *first.exe*. If you are working on a Unix system, you may have to use two commands – the first to compile your code; the second to link it to built-in chunks of code and turn it into an executable program. (The commands used depend upon the system.) The resulting file will be called *first*. In either case, when the program is run, you will see this on screen.

Hello World

Not very exciting, but you have to start somewhere.

Tip

Before you go any further, you must learn how to use your editor (to write the code) and compiler. If you are using Turbo Pascal, turn to Chapter 8 to find out about its system.

The basic structure

At the simplest, a program takes this shape:

```
program title;

begin
    statement;
    statement;
    statement;
end.
```

The important things to notice here are:

- Programs always start with the word **program** followed by the name. The name must be a single word – no spaces or punctuation – but can normally be of any length.

- The start of the active part of the program is marked by **begin**.

- The end of the active part is marked by **end**.

- **program**, **begin** and **end** are all *reserved words* – ones with special meaning. They can be written in lower case or capitals.

- The full stop at the end is essential.

- A program can contain any number of *statements*.

- A statement will usually be on a line by itself, but can be spread over several.

- Each statement is separated from the next by a semi-colon. This is normally written at the end of the line.

- To make the program easier to read, lines may be indented. This is more useful in more complex programs, where different levels of indents can help to bring out the structure.

- Whether and how far you indent is entirely up to you. The compiler ignores all spaces and tabs in your code.

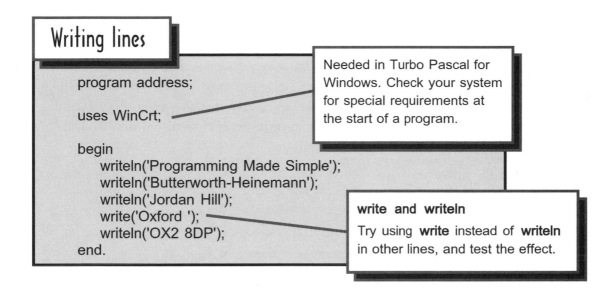

Writing lines

```
program address;

uses WinCrt;

begin
    writeln('Programming Made Simple');
    writeln('Butterworth-Heinemann');
    writeln('Jordan Hill');
    write('Oxford ');
    writeln('OX2 8DP');
end.
```

Needed in Turbo Pascal for Windows. Check your system for special requirements at the start of a program.

write and writeln
Try using **write** instead of **writeln** in other lines, and test the effect.

Use your system's editor to create an address program, on the lines of the one shown here. The text can be anything you like – you don't have to write to us. The program introduces the reserved words **write** and **writeln**.

write('text')   This displays on screen whatever is in the curved brackets, leaving the cursor after the last character. Anything written next will appear immediately after it. write can display numbers, text or data stored in memory. Any text must be enclosed in single quotes.

writeln('text') This also displays something on screen, but then moves the cursor to the start of the next line.

When compiled and run, the program should display:

```
Programming Made Simple
Butterworth-Heinemann
Jordan Hill
Oxford OX2 8DP
```

Writing on screen

Let's look a bit closer at **writeln**. This is a *procedure* – a command that performs an operation on the data that is passed to it. The *data* can be actual text or numbers, variables or functions that produce suitable text or number values. You can output several items of data in one writeln – separate them with commas.

Try this program to see how text, integers and decimal values are displayed on your screen.

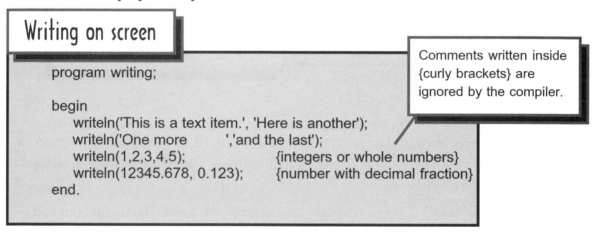

Writing on screen

```
program writing;

begin
    writeln('This is a text item.', 'Here is another');
    writeln('One more        ','and the last');
    writeln(1,2,3,4,5);                {integers or whole numbers}
    writeln(12345.678, 0.123);      {number with decimal fraction}
end.
```

> Comments written inside {curly brackets} are ignored by the compiler.

The resulting display should be like this:

```
This is a text item.Here is another
 One more        and the last
12345
1.2345678000E+04  1.230000000E-01
```

● Where there are several items in a writeln, they are displayed immediately after each other unless you include spaces inside the quotes.

● Decimal values – called real numbers in Pascal – are displayed in scientific format.

Both of these aspects of the display can be changed.

writeln parameters

writeln can take *parameters* (also called *arguments*) to change the way that it displays data. There are two parameters, controlling *field width* and *decimal places*.

The field width parameter

This sets the width of the space that the data is to be displayed in. The parameter is written immediately after the data item, separated by a colon (:). The width is measured in characters, and the data is aligned to the right of the field. e.g.

writeln('Centre stage':46)

This will set *'Centre stage'* on screen with the final *'e'* at column 46 – effectively centering the text on an 80-column screen.

Decimal place parameter

This can only be used on real numbers. It makes the display into the more readable digits.decimals pattern, and specifies how many decimal places to show.

This is always the second parameter – you must therefore set a field width value first. e.g.

writeln(123.4567:10:2)

displays

123.46

with the final 6 at the 10th column.

If you want the number to be aligned to the left, or appear directly after a piece of text, set the field width to 0. e.g.

writeln('The answer is ',42.1834:0:3)

This produces:

The answer is 42.183

Take note

write is used in exactly the same as **writeln.**

Field widths

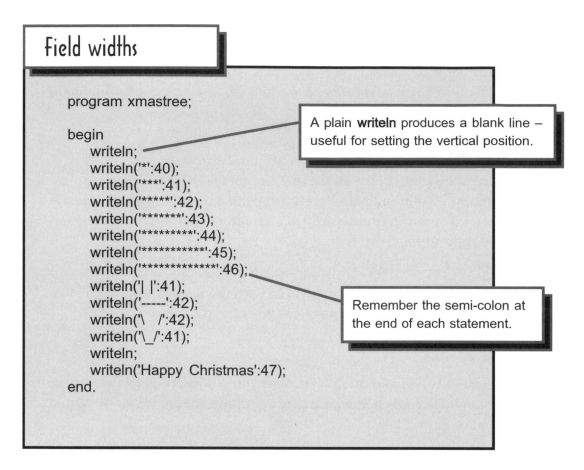

```
program xmastree;

begin
    writeln;
    writeln('*':40);
    writeln('***':41);
    writeln('*****':42);
    writeln('*******':43);
    writeln('*********':44);
    writeln('***********':45);
    writeln('*************':46);
    writeln('| |':41);
    writeln('-----':42);
    writeln('\   /':42);
    writeln('\_/':41);
    writeln;
    writeln('Happy Christmas':47);
end.
```

A plain **writeln** produces a blank line — useful for setting the vertical position.

Remember the semi-colon at the end of each statement.

This program shows how you can use the field width parameters to line up text on a screen.

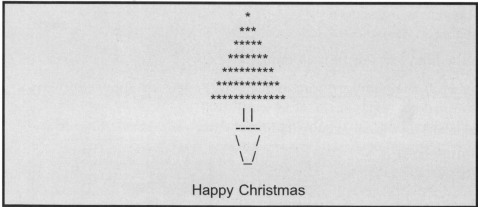

```
              *
             ***
            *****
           *******
          *********
         ***********
        *************
              | |
             -----
             \   /
              \_/
```

Happy Christmas

If it's not December when you read this, work out a more seasonal design of your own!

```
program writepars;

begin
    writeln('Using Field Width Parameters':50);
    {text ends at column 50}

    writeln('Left','Centre':30,'Right':40);
    {Display 3 items across the screen}

    writeln(12345:10);
    {Last digit will be in column 10}

    writeln(12345.678:10:2);
    {End at column 10, show 2 decimal places}

    writeln(1.2345678:0:4);
    {Start of line,  show 4 decimal places}
end.
```

This second example demonstrates the use of both field width and decimal place parameters. Type it in, compile it and run it. The output should be:

```
                    Using Field Width Parameters
Left                      Centre                            Right
        12345
    12345.68
1.2346
```

Change the numbers and the values of the parameters. Compile and run the program again, to see the effect of the changes.

Variables and types of data

If you want to handle any data while the program is running, you must set up *variables*. These are areas of memory, identified by a name written into the code. When setting up a variable, you must say what type of data is to be stored there, as different types require different amounts of memory.

Data types

Pascal recognises several types of data. The main ones are:

char　　A single character, which can be a letter, symbol or digit – in fact, any character from the ASCII set. (See page 29.) This normally takes a single byte of memory.

integer　A whole number, in the range from –32,768 to +32,767. These take 2 bytes of memory.

longint　A whole number in the range –2,147,483,648 to +2,147,483,647. Long integers require 4 bytes of memory.

real　　Any number, with or without a decimal fraction, from:

0.000,000,000,000,000,000,000,000,000,000,000,003
to
+1,700,000,000,000,000,000,000,000,000,000,000,000,000
which should cope with the data you are collecting with your electron microscope or radio telescope!

boolean These can only store the values 'TRUE' or 'FALSE'. Boolean variables are generally used to store the results of logical tests. (See page 40.)

Take note

Turbo Pascal has a 'string' data type, for storing words or phrases. Standard Pascal does not have this, and special techniques are needed for handling strings of text. (See page 56.)

variable names

Names must be single words, but can normally be of any length. An ideal name is one that shows clearly what it is used to store, but is reasonably short and easy to type. You cannot use reserved words – those that have a special meaning in Pascal – or numbers as variable names. If the name needs two or more words, you can run them all together, separate them by underlines or capitalise the start of each – just do not use spaces or punctuation!

Acceptable	Unacceptable	
total	begin	(reserved word)
x	12	(number value)
a1	Taxable.Amount	(punctuation)
FirstName	pen colour	(space)
VatToPay	poiuyt	(meaningless – you'll forget it!)

var

This reserved word is used to mark the start of the area in which variables are *declared* (created). This must be at the top of the program, as the variables must be set up before the rest of the code can be compiled. To declare a variable, you simply give its name and its type, like this:

```
var
    n1, n2   : integer;
    number   : integer;
    bignum   : real;
    initial  : char;
    YesNo    : boolean;
```

● You can declare any number of variables – *of the same type* – in the same line. To keep the program readable, only do this where the variables are closely related.

● Punctuation! There is a colon between the variable name and its type, and a semi-colon at the end of the line. If there are several variable names in the line, they are separated by commas.

● The declaration block is usually indented, for readability.

Variable := value

There are two ways of storing data in variables: they can come in from outside (through the keyboard or from disk), or values can be assigned from within the program. Let's start with the latter.

Values are assigned to variables with the operator ':=' – colon followed by equals. The variable name sits to the left, and on the right is an actual value, another variable, a function, or an expression that produces a value of the right type. This expression can include values, variables and functions. e.g.

```
number := 99;
answer := a + b * 2;
angle := sin(y);
status := 'M';
total := total + next;
```

- In the second example, *answer*, *a* and *b* would normally all be integers, or all reals.

- In the third, angle must be a real, because the *sin()* function produces a real value.

- In the last example, the computer will look up the current value of *total*, add *next* to it, then store the result back in *total*.

- Some systems will set number variables to 0 when they are created. Others simply allocate memory space, and the memory may have old values lurking in it. To avoid problems, always zero counters and totals early on in the program. e.g.

```
counter := 0;
```

will guarantee that the later line:

```
counter := counter + 1;
```

keeps proper track of the count.

Take note

Fixed values can be stored in constants — see page 18.

12

```
program valuevar;

var
    a,b,c    :    integer;
    decimal  :    real;
    letter   :    char;
    YesNo    :    boolean;

begin
    a := 2;
    b := 3;
    c := a + b;
    decimal := 9.99;
    letter := 'X';
    YesNo := TRUE;

    writeln('a = ',a,' b = ',b,' and c = ',c);
    writeln('Decimal holds ',decimal:0:2);
    writeln('The letter is ',letter);
    writeln('The value of YesNo is ',YesNo);
end.
```

When the program is compiled and run, you should see this:

```
a = 2 b = 3 and c = 5
Decimal holds 9.99
The letter is X
The value of YesNo is TRUE
```

Copy the **writeln** lines to the start of the program, before values are assigned to the variables, and see what they display there. Does your system zero the numbers automatically?

Inputs

At its simplest, the **readln** procedure waits for a user to type in data and press [Enter], then passes the data to a variable. As it does not prompt the user for data, you should normally put a **write** or **writeln** statement before it so that your users knows it's time to type.

write is generally better than **writeln**, as it leaves the cursor on the same line as the prompt – include a space at the end of the prompt text for a neater display. When the user presses [Enter], the cursor will move down to the next line.

This next program takes in two numbers and displays their total.

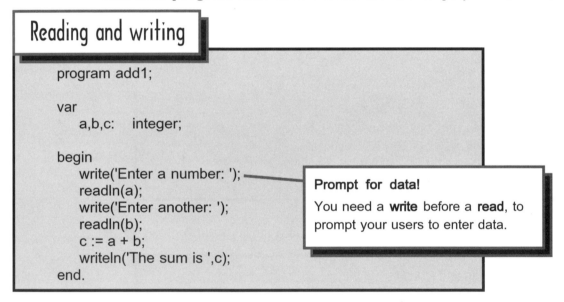

Reading and writing

```
program add1;

var
    a,b,c:    integer;

begin
    write('Enter a number: ');
    readln(a);
    write('Enter another: ');
    readln(b);
    c := a + b;
    writeln('The sum is ',c);
end.
```

Prompt for data!
You need a **write** before a **read**, to prompt your users to enter data.

When compiled and run, the screen should look like this.

```
Enter a number: 5
Enter another: 7
The sum is 12
```

(The user's inputs are shown in **bold**.)

read and readln

Like **write** and **writeln**, **read** and **readln** are almost – but not quite – identical. In theory, **readln** waits for the [Enter] key to be pressed before passing data, while **read** passes data into the variable immediately. In practice, what happens depends more upon your system. Use the following program to test the difference.

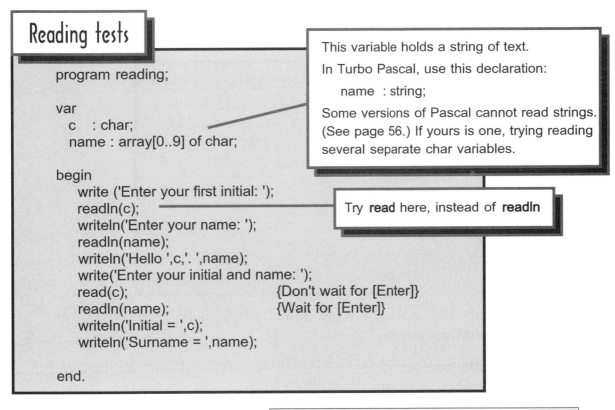

Reading tests

```
program reading;

var
   c    : char;
   name : array[0..9] of char;

begin
    write ('Enter your first initial: ');
    readln(c);
    writeln('Enter your name: ');
    readln(name);
    writeln('Hello ',c,'. ',name);
    write('Enter your initial and name: ');
    read(c);                  {Don't wait for [Enter]}
    readln(name);             {Wait for [Enter]}
    writeln('Initial = ',c);
    writeln('Surname = ',name);

end.
```

This variable holds a string of text.

In Turbo Pascal, use this declaration:

> name : string;

Some versions of Pascal cannot read strings. (See page 56.) If yours is one, trying reading several separate char variables.

Try **read** here, instead of **readln**

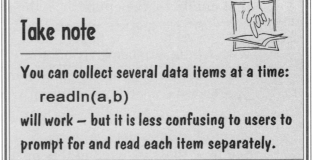

Take note

You can collect several data items at a time:

   readln(a,b)

will work – but it is less confusing to users to prompt for and read each item separately.

Arithmetic operators

We have seen that Pascal recognises two main types of numbers – integers and those with decimals (real). These operators are used in the same way with both types:

+   plus
-         minus
*   multiply

Type in this program, compile and run it.

Simple sums

```
program sums;
var
    a,b,c  :   real;

begin
    Write('Enter first number: ');
    Readln(a);
    Write('Enter second number: ');
    Readln(b);
    c := a + b;
    Writeln(a:0:2,' + ',b:0:2,' = ',c:0:2);
end.
```

- Edit the **c :=** line and run it again to test subtraction and multiplication.

- Change the type from **real** to **integer**, removing the decimal place parameters from the **writeln**.

When you turn to division, the two types are treated differently. With real numbers, the operator is the standard division symbol:

/   division

With whole number division, there are two answers from each sum – the dividend (how many times) and the remainder. This needs two operators:

div   dividend (how many times it divides)
mod   remainder

See how they are used in this next program.

Division

```
program division;
var
    a,b,c,d: integer;
    e,f,g:      real;

begin
    {integer division}
    write('Enter first number: ');
    readln(a);
    write('Enter second number: ');
    readln(b);
    c := a DIV b;
    d := a MOD b;
    writeln(a,' divided by ',b,' is ',c,' remainder ',d);

    {real division}
    write('Enter first real number: ');
    readln(e);
    write('Enter second real number: ');
    readln(f);
    g := e / f;
    writeln(e:0:2,' divided by ',f:0:2,' is ',g:0:2);
end.
```

Tip

In Turbo Pascal, you can mix reals and integers in the same calculation, though the answer will always be a real value. In standard Pascal, if you want to mix different types, they must be converted to the same type before calculating with them — see page 20.

Constants

Constants, like variables, are places in which you can store values. The difference between them is clear from their names – the values in *variables* can be *varied* during a program's execution, while *constants* stay *constant*.

Constants are defined at the top of program, in a section marked const, before variable declaration. The rules for constant names are the same as for variable names, though using capital letters has become a generally accepted convention.

To define a constant, give its name and the number or text value that it stands for. You can see this in the simple invoicing program shown opposite. The VAT percentage is stored as the constant VAT, defined at the top of the program.

```
const
    VAT = 0.175;
```

When the compiler reaches the line:

```
vatamount := topay * VAT;
```

it simply substitutes the value for the constant's name, treating the line as if it read;

```
vatamount := topay * 0.175;
```

As constants' values do not change, you might ask why bother with them? Why not just write the values directly into the program code? In fact, there are two very good reasons for using constants:

● constants make your code more readable;

● constants make your programs easier to update.

If this had been a fully worked invoicing program, there could well have been half a dozen or more occurrences of the VAT percentage within the code. If the VAT percentage is changed in the next Budget, then with the value defined as a constant, it will take only a moment to change that to update the program. If the actual value had been used, then updating the program would involve tracking down and changing each occurrence. This is not just slower, it also leaves more opportunities for bugs to creep into the program.

Using constants

```
program constants;

const
    VAT = 0.175;
    discount= 0.10;
    title = 'Invoice';

var
    price: real;
    moneyoff : real;
    topay : rcal;
    vatamount: real;
    vatinc : real;
    total : real;

begin
    writeln(title);
    price := 200;
    moneyoff := price * discount;
    topay := price - moneyoff;
    vatamount := topay * VAT;
    total := topay + vatamount;
    writeln('Price of goods = ',price:0:2);
    writeln('Discount at ',discount:0:2,' = ',moneyoff:0:2);
    writeln('Total exclusive of VAT = ',topay:0:2);
    writeln('VAT at ',VAT*100:0:1,'% = ',vatamount:0:2);
    writeln('Total due = ',total:0:2);
end.
```

const marks the start of the constant definition area – put this before the **var** area..

You can store text or number values in constants.

The effect of
...VAT*100:0:1,'%...
is to make the value appear as a percentage.

Sample output

```
Invoice
Price of goods = 200.00
Discount at 0.10 = 20.00
Total exclusive of VAT = 180.00
VAT at 17.5% = 31.50
Total due = 211.50
```

Number functions

Pascal is equipped with a set of *functions* that can manipulate numbers in various ways. Among these are some for converting real numbers to integers and similar operations.

trunc(real)   extracts the integer part of the number and ignores the decimal fraction. The result is an integer.

round(real)   converts a real to the nearest integer, rounding up or down as appropriate

int(real)   like trunc(), this extracts the integer part, but the result is still a *real* value.

frac(real)   extracts the decimal fraction.

conv(integer)   converts an integer into a real. This function does not exist in Turbo Pascal where integers are automatically converted to reals, if necessary.

You can use a function in any situation where you could use a value or variable of the same type. e.g.

```
num := trunc(x);
writeln('The nearest whole is ',round(x));
x := conv(num) / 1.2;
```

In all of these, *num* is an integer and *x* is a real.

Take note

When an expression contains a mixture of arithmetic operators and/or functions – e.g. 3.14 * SQR(X) + 10, they are evaluated in this order:

```
()
functions
* / DIV MOD
+ -
```

These conversion functions are illustrated in the next program. Type it in, and run it several times, to test their effects on a range of values.

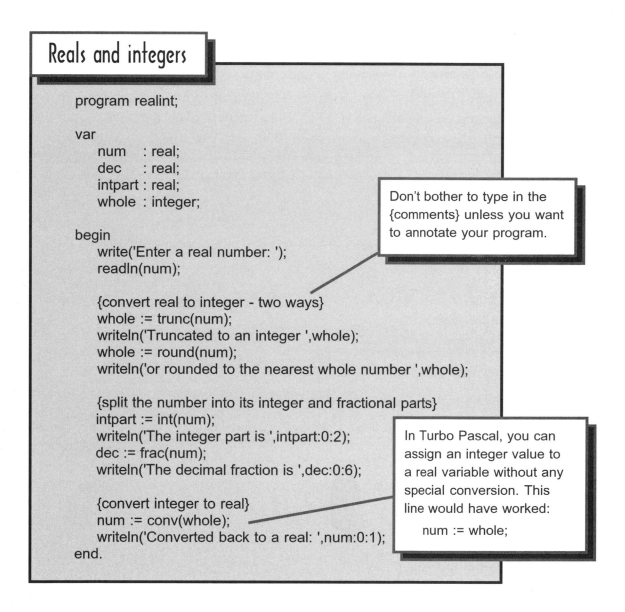

Reals and integers

```
program realint;

var
    num    : real;
    dec    : real;
    intpart : real;
    whole  : integer;

begin
    write('Enter a real number: ');
    readln(num);

    {convert real to integer - two ways}
    whole := trunc(num);
    writeln('Truncated to an integer ',whole);
    whole := round(num);
    writeln('or rounded to the nearest whole number ',whole);

    {split the number into its integer and fractional parts}
    intpart := int(num);
    writeln('The integer part is ',intpart:0:2);
    dec := frac(num);
    writeln('The decimal fraction is ',dec:0:6);

    {convert integer to real}
    num := conv(whole);
    writeln('Converted back to a real: ',num:0:1);
end.
```

Don't bother to type in the {comments} unless you want to annotate your program.

In Turbo Pascal, you can assign an integer value to a real variable without any special conversion. This line would have worked:

```
num := whole;
```

Exercises

1   Write a program using field width parameters, to display your name and address in staggered format, with each line starting 4 places further to the right.

2   Write a program to take in two real numbers and display the results of adding, subtracting, multiyplying and dividing them. The results should show 2 decimal places.

3   A painter needs to know the quantities of paint to buy to decorate the 4 walls and ceiling of a room. 1 litre of new 'Once-over' paint will cover 5 square metres.Write a program that asks the height, width and length of the room and calculates the amounts needed for the ceiling and the walls. (Ignore the holes caused by windows and doors!)

2 Program flow

for loops

'Program flow' refers to the order in which a program's instructions are carried out. So far, all the example programs have run straight through a sequence, then stopped. There are few practical uses for such simple programs. The addition of loops and branches makes programs far more useful and powerful.

The **for** loop probably offers the simplest way to repeat a set of instructions. The basic shape is this:

> **for** *variable* := *start_value* **to** *end_value* **do**
> *statement or block of statements;*

When the program reaches this point for the first time, the *variable* is given the *start_value*. The following statement (or block of statements – see next page) is executed and the flow loops back to the **for** line. The *variable* is incremented by 1, and the statement executed again. The flow continues to go round the loop until the *variable* reaches the *end_value*.

This next program, for example, asks the user for a number, then displays the multiples of that number, from 1 times to 12 times.

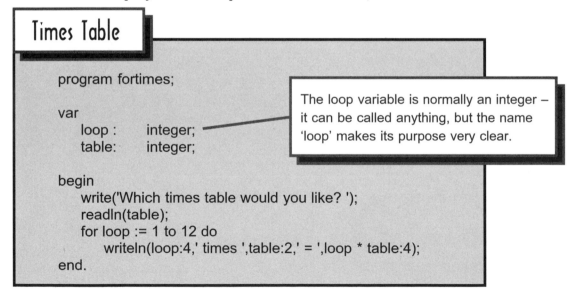

Times Table

```
program fortimes;

var
     loop :      integer;
     table:      integer;

begin
     write('Which times table would you like? ');
     readln(table);
     for loop := 1 to 12 do
          writeln(loop:4,' times ',table:2,' = ',loop * table:4);
end.
```

The loop variable is normally an integer – it can be called anything, but the name 'loop' makes its purpose very clear.

Type it in and test it. Try different start and end values and note their effects. What happens if the end value is less than the start value?

begin ... end blocks

You would normally want to loop through a set of instructions – rather than a single statement. You can do this by enclosing them in the reserved words **begin** and **end**. The only difference between using the pair here and using them to enclose the whole program, is that the program's **end** is followed by a full stop whereas a set of statements finished with a semi-colon.

For example, we can extend the last example to display the power of the number, as well as its multiple, each time through the loop.

Blocks of statements

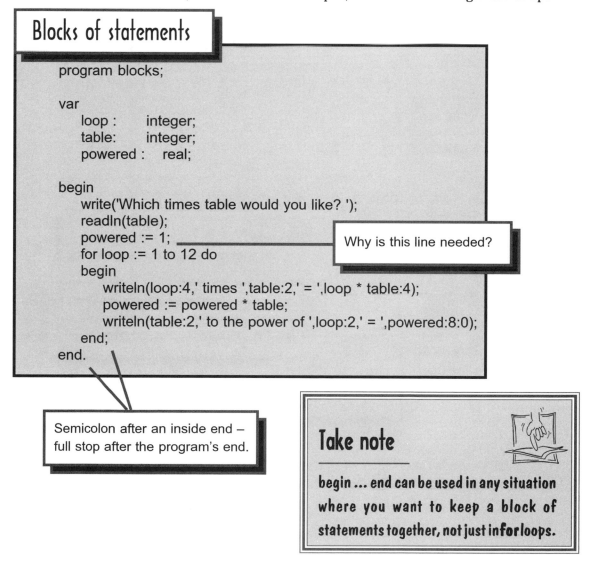

```
program blocks;

var
    loop :      integer;
    table:      integer;
    powered :   real;

begin
    write('Which times table would you like? ');
    readln(table);
    powered := 1;
    for loop := 1 to 12 do
    begin
        writeln(loop:4,' times ',table:2,' = ',loop * table:4);
        powered := powered * table;
        writeln(table:2,' to the power of ',loop:2,' = ',powered:8:0);
    end;
end.
```

Why is this line needed?

Semicolon after an inside end – full stop after the program's end.

Take note

begin ... end can be used in any situation where you want to keep a block of statements together, not just in **for** loops.

Varying loop values

The number of times that a **for** loop is iterated (repeated) is determined by the start and end values, but these do not have to be decided at design time. If either or both values are held in variables, they can be set by the program's user or calculated during its run. You can see this in the next example. It adds up a set of numbers – having first asked the user how many numbers are to be added.

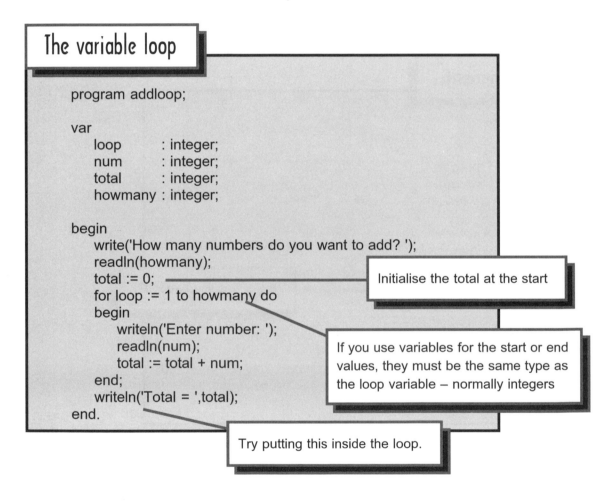

The variable loop

```
program addloop;

var
    loop      : integer;
    num       : integer;
    total     : integer;
    howmany : integer;

begin
    write('How many numbers do you want to add? ');
    readln(howmany);
    total := 0;
    for loop := 1 to howmany do
    begin
        writeln('Enter number: ');
        readln(num);
        total := total + num;
    end;
    writeln('Total = ',total);
end.
```

Initialise the total at the start

If you use variables for the start or end values, they must be the same type as the loop variable – normally integers

Try putting this inside the loop.

This idea is taken further in the next example. Here we have two loops, one inside the other, and the end value of the inner loop it determined by the current value of the outer loop.

What do you think this program will do?

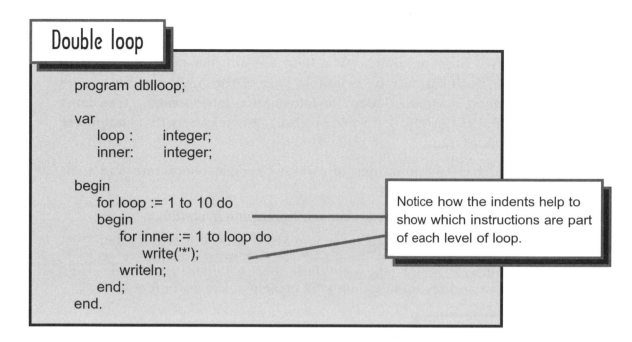

Double loop

```
program dblloop;

var
    loop :      integer;
    inner:      integer;

begin
    for loop := 1 to 10 do
    begin
        for inner := 1 to loop do
            write('*');
        writeln;
    end;
end.
```

Notice how the indents help to show which instructions are part of each level of loop.

downto

Here's one last variation that is perhaps more interesting than useful. Instead of **for...to...do** you can have **for ... downto... do**. This decrements the variable each time round the loop. NASA find this very handy!

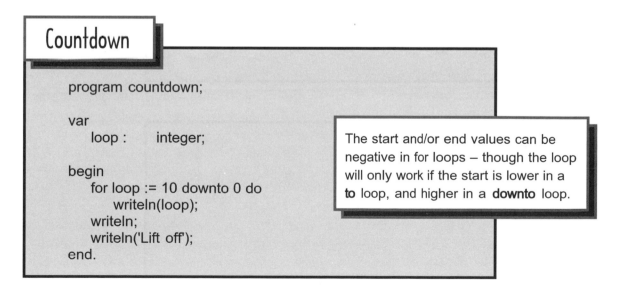

Countdown

```
program countdown;

var
    loop :      integer;

begin
    for loop := 10 downto 0 do
        writeln(loop);
    writeln;
    writeln('Lift off');
end.
```

The start and/or end values can be negative in for loops – though the loop will only work if the start is lower in a **to** loop, and higher in a **downto** loop.

Loops and characters

The two little programs given here are not just more examples of loops. Both display the printable part of the ASCII set. This – the American Standard Codes for Information Interchange – translates characters (letters, digits and symbols) into numbers that computers can understand.

Pascal has two functions to switch between characters and their ASCII number codes:

chr(n)   turns a number into its character; e.g. chr(65) is 'A'

ord(c)   turns a character into an ASCII code; e.g. ord('A') is 65

They are both very short, and both produce identical outputs. Type them in and try them – then look closely at the second one.

Characters from codes

```
program ascloop;

var
  n : integer;

begin
    for n := 32 to 126 do
        write(n:4,chr(n):4);
end.
```

Codes from characters

```
program charloop;

var
  c : char;

begin
    for c := ' ' to '~' do
        write(ord(c):4,c:4);
end.
```

32		33	!	34	"	35	#	36	$	37	%
38	&	39	'	40	(	41	)	42	*	43	+
44	,	45	-	46	.	47	/	48	0	49	1
50	2	51	3	52	4	53	5	54	6	55	7
56	8	57	9	58	:	59	;	60	<	61	=
62	>	63	?	64	@	65	A	66	B	67	C
68	D	69	E	70	F	71	G	72	H	73	I
74	J	75	K	76	L	77	M	78	N	79	O
80	P	81	Q	82	R	83	S	84	T	85	U
86	V	87	W	88	X	89	Y	90	Z	91	[
92	\	93	]	94	^	95	_	96	`	97	a
98	b	99	c	100	d	101	e	102	f	103	g
104	h	105	i	106	j	107	k	108	l	109	m
110	n	111	o	112	p	113	q	114	r	115	s
116	t	117	u	118	v	119	w	120	x	121	y
122	z	123	{	124			125	}	126	~		

The full ASCII set goes from 0 to 255, but those below 32 are not printable (they are mainly used for screen and printer control), 127 is backspace and from 128 upwards there are several alternative sets.

Counting in chars

The loop variable in the second example was a *char*. Chars, like integers, are *ordinal* types – you can count through them one at a time. Real values are not ordinal as they can have decimal fractions. As you will see on page 65, you can create other ordinal types. It is possible, for instance, to create a valid loop that reads:

    for day := monday to friday do
        ...

Tip

If you are having trouble with errors, turn to Debugging, page 46.

repeat ... until

Here is another way to loop, but in this case, the number of iterations is not fixed. With this structure, the flow passes through the block then keeps looping back to the start until a value entered by the user, or calculated by the program, satisfies its exit condition. The basic shape is:

repeat
    statement(s)
until *exit_test*

- If there are several *statements* in the loop, you do not need **begin ... end** to hold them together. The **repeat** and **until** words act as brackets to enclose the block.

- The *exit_test* will usually compare a variable with a value or with another variable.

In this example program, the flow loops round, taking in and adding a number to the total, until the user enters '0'.

Repeated addition

```
program repeatadd;

var
    num    : integer;
    total  : integer;

begin
    repeat
        writeln('Enter number or 0 to end: ');
        readln(num);
        total := total + num;
        writeln('Total = ',total);
    until num = 0;
end.
```

Which equals?

Note the difference. When testing a value (is it equal to?), use a plain = sign.

When assigning a value (make it equal to), add a colon before the sign (:=)

30

Where a program offers a number of options to its users, the selection is often handled through a menu. If this is enclosed in a repeat loop – and an 'exit' option included in the menu – the program flow will return to the menu from each option, until the user wants to quit.

Running from a menu

```
program menu;

var
   choice : char;

begin
   repeat
         writeln('Start a new file......1');
         writeln('Save the file..........2');
         writeln('Load a file.............3');
         writeln('Exit.......................4');
         readln(choice);
   ...
   ...
      until choice = '4'
end.
```

The missing lines would deal with choices 1 to 3.

Notice in this example, that the menu choices are numbers, but that they are read into a *char* variable. It works perfectly well, as only a single digit is wanted, and this can be treated as a character. This is a neat solution to two problems:

● If the user enters a non-number when the program trying to read into an integer or real variable, the system crashes. (There are ways to take in numbers safely – see page 98.)

● If you select by letter ('O to Open a new file', etc), you have to cope with both lower case and capital letters. This requires slightly more complex testing – see page 36.

Both problems are soluble, but this approach is far simpler.

while loops

while loops are used in much the same way as repeat loops, but there is one major difference between them – while loops are tested on entry; repeat loops are tested on exit. As a result, the statements in a repeat loop are always executed at least once, but those in a while loop may not be executed at all.

Here's the basic shape – compare it with the shape of the repeat loop on page 30.

while (*test*) **do**
    statement or block of statements;

- You must give an initial value to the variable being tested, even though it may be overwritten as soon as the loop statements are executed.

- If you want to loop round several statements, they must be enclosed in begin and end, as with the **if** structure.

Look for these points in this example program.

The while loop

```
program while1;

var
    num   : integer;
    total : integer;

begin
    num := -1;
    while num <> 0 do
    begin
        writeln('Enter number (0 to end): ');
        readln(num);
        total := total + num;
        writeln('Total = ',total);
    end;
end.
```

Any non-zero value will do here – the important thing in this case is to ensure that the looped code is executed at least once.

A common use for **while** loops is to collect input where the user has failed to enter suitable data on first asking. Here's a trivial example.

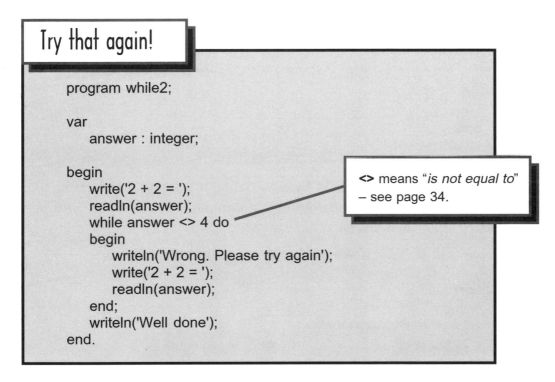

Try that again!

```
program while2;

var
    answer : integer;

begin
    write('2 + 2 = ');
    readln(answer);
    while answer <> 4 do
    begin
        writeln('Wrong. Please try again');
        write('2 + 2 = ');
        readln(answer);
    end;
    writeln('Well done');
end.
```

<> means "*is not equal to*" – see page 34.

For a more realistic example, look at the menu program on page 31. What happens if your user enters a number that is not on the menu? At the moment, the program would simply redisplay the menu and ask for a choice again. A neater solution is to use a while loop to check the user's choice and ask – clearly, but firmly – for a suitable value.

```
    ...
    readln(choice);
    while (choice  < '1') and (choice > '4') do
    begin
        writeln('Between 1 and 4 only please! Enter your choice: ');
        readln(choice)
    end;
```

That rather complicated while line will make more sense after you have looked at logical operators (page 36).

Branching with if

Loops make programs powerful, giving them the ability to process masses of data. Branches make them flexible, allowing them to vary their actions in response to incoming data. The simplest form of branch uses the **if ... then** structure. This is its basic syntax:

if *test* **then** *statement*;

or where there are several statements:

if *test*
    then
    begin
        statements;
    end;

The *test* checks the value held by a variable. **if** the *test* proves true, **then** the program performs the following *statement(s)*. If the test does not prove true, the statements are ignored.

●   Note that there is a semi-colon at the end of the structure.

Comparison operators

The tests use these operators:

=	is equal to	**<>**	is not equal to
<=	is less than or equal to	**>=**	is greater than or equal to

The tests can be applied to any type of variable – though special care is needed with strings or arrays of chars (see page 96), and boolean variables are treated slightly differently (see page 40).

When testing char variables, 'less than' and 'greater than' apply to the (numeric) ASCII codes of characters.

Some examples of valid tests:

```
if x > 99          {true if the value in x is greater than 99}
if letter <= 'Z'   {true if a capital letter or other character
                    lower down in the ASCII set}
if ans <> correct  {true if the variables do not match}
```

The next example shows the use of the '=' operator in if ... then tests. It takes in two numbers and then performs the chosen arithmetic operation on them.

The if calculator

```
program calc1;

var
    num1, num2, answer  : real;
    op   :    char;

begin
    write('Enter first number: ');
    readln(num1);
    write('Enter next number: ');
    readln(num2);
    write('What sort of sum(+-*/) ');
    readln(op);
    if op = '+' then answer := num1 + num2;
    if op = '-' then answer := num1 - num2;
    if op = '*' then answer := num1 * num2;
    if op = '/' then answer := num1 / num2;
    writeln('The answer is ',answer:0:3);
end.
```

Tip

These little test programs only go through once each time you run them. If you want to keep them looping round, while you test them out, add the lines:

repeat

after the begin, and

until false

before the end. The program will then run forever! To stop it, press [Ctrl]-[C] on PCs, or [Ctrl]-[D] on Unix machines.

Logical operators

The comparison operators will test a variable against one value at a time, but you will often want to check if a variable falls into a range of values, or is one of several possibilities. This is where the logical operators come into play. There are three: AND, OR and NOT.

AND links two tests. The expression is true if both of the tests are true.

if (x >= 20) AND (x <= 30) then...

The expression is true for all values of x from 20 to 30 inclusive.

OR also links two tests. In this case, the expression is true if *either or both* of the tests are true.

if (reply = 'y') OR (reply = 'Y') then...

This is true whether the user has typed a capital or lower case 'y'.

A logical expression can have more than two tests and can include both AND and OR. In mixed expressions, AND is evaluated before OR, unless you use brackets. Anything in brackets is evaluated first.

if (x >= 20) AND (x <= 30) OR (y > 100) then...

For this to be true, the x value must be between 20 and 30, or the y value over 100 – in which case the x value is irrelevant.

if ((reply = 'y') OR (reply = 'Y')) AND (saved = TRUE) then...

This proves true only if the user has entered 'Y' (either capital or lower case) and the *saved* variable is set to TRUE. What would happen if the brackets where removed from that first OR expression?

NOT reverses the truth of a test. It is rarely used on a single test:

NOT (x = 100)

is the same as

x <> 100

But it can make compound tests more readable:

NOT ((letter >='a') and (letter <='z'))

is a neat way of saying 'not a lower case letter'.

Some versions of Pascal support **XOR**, which gives a true result if either one or the other – but not both – of a pair are true.

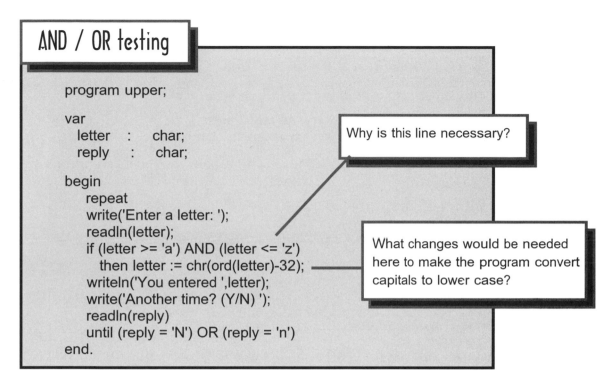

AND / OR testing

```
program upper;

var
  letter  :   char;
  reply   :   char;

begin
  repeat
    write('Enter a letter: ');
    readln(letter);
    if (letter >= 'a') AND (letter <= 'z')
      then letter := chr(ord(letter)-32);
    writeln('You entered ',letter);
    write('Another time? (Y/N) ');
    readln(reply)
  until (reply = 'N') OR (reply = 'n')
end.
```

Why is this line necessary?

What changes would be needed here to make the program convert capitals to lower case?

This program converts lower case to capitals. It does this by finding their ASCII code, with ORD(), subtracting 32, and converting back to a character with CHR(). e.g. ORD('a') is 97. 97 - 32 = 65. CHR(65) is 'A'.

Notice the use of AND when checking that the letter is in the right range, and the use of OR for accepting a lower case or capital letter as the reply.

Try it. When run, it should give output like this.

```
Enter a letter: q
You entered Q
Another time? (Y/N) y
Enter a letter: W
You entered W
Another time? (Y/N) y
Enter a letter: 3
You entered 3
Another time? (Y/N) n
```

Multiple branching

What happens if you want to perform a different set of actions if a test proves true and another if it proves false?

With the simple **if ... then**, you need two separate tests.

```
if age < 18 then writeln('Sorry, no admittance.');
if age >= 18 then writeln('Welcome to our club');
```

There is an extended form of **if ...** which handles these situations neatly:

```
if test
    then statements-if-true
    else statements-if-false;
```

For example:

```
if age < 18
    then writeln('Sorry, no admittance.')
    else writeln('Welcome to our club');
```

Both forms are used in this next program. It works out the correct form of address to suit a person's age, sex and marital status. This tree diagram shows the branching plan.

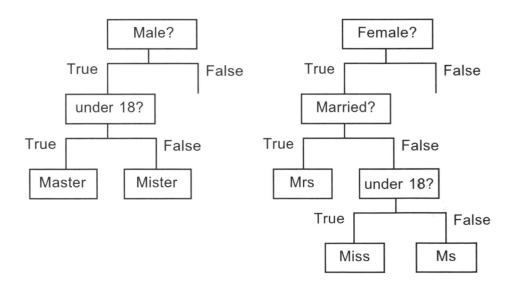

if ... then ... else

```
program titles;

var
    age    : integer;
    sex    : char;
    status : char;

begin
    write('Enter age in years: ');
    readln(age);
    write('Sex (M/F): ');
    readln(sex);
    write('Marital status (M)arried, (S)ingle: ');
    readln(status);
    if (sex = 'M') or (sex = 'm')                    {male}
        then if age < 18
                then Writeln('call him Master')      {young}
                else Writeln('call him Mr');
    if (sex = 'F') or (sex = 'f')                    {female}
        then if (status = 'M') or (status = 'm')     {married}
                then Writeln('call her Mrs')
                else if age < 18
                        then Writeln('call her Miss')  {young}
                        else Writeln('call her Ms');
end.
```

What would you have to do to make the program match this plan?

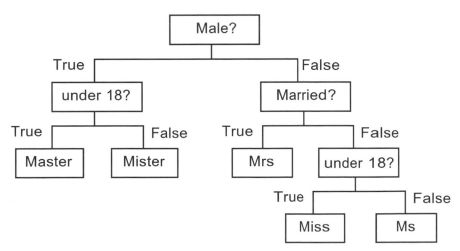

Boolean variables

Boolean variables can only take the values 'True' and 'False' so you can only test if they are equal or not equal to either of those. In fact, a full comparison is not needed.

    if finished

has exactly the same effect as:

    if finished = true

Similarly, you can write

    if not finished

instead of

    if finished = false

Booleans are generally used for storing the result of a test and passing it to another part of the program. This approach is common in **while** and **repeat** loops, especially where the control variable is tested early on in a long set of statements. For example:

Boolean repeat loop

```
program boolex;

var
   done  : boolean;
   num   : integer;
   total : integer;

begin
   done := false;
   repeat
      writeln('Enter number  or 0 to end: ');
      readln(num);
      if num = 0 then done := true;
      total := total + num;
      writeln('Total = ',total);
   until done;
   end.
```

This loop could equally well have ended:

    until num = 0

40

Because booleans can be tested so simply, they can make complex expressions more readable. Here's the form of address program re-written using boolean variables.

Booleans in expressions

```
program b_titles;

var
    age    : integer;
    sex    : char;
    status : char;
    male, young, married : boolean;

begin
{get data}
    write('Enter age in years: ');
    readln(age);
    write('Sex (M/F): ');
    readln(sex);
    write('Marital status (M)arried, (S)ingle: ');
    readln(status);
{test and store results}
    if age < 18                        {young?}
        then young := true
        else young := false;
    if (sex = 'M') or (sex = 'm')       {male?}
        then male := true
        else male := false;
    if (status = 'M') or (status = 'm')  {married?}
        then married := true
        else married := false;
{output appropriate form of address}
    if male and young then writeln('call him Master');
    if male and not young then writeln('call him Mr');
    if not male and married then writeln('call her Mrs');
    if not male and not married and young then writeln('call her Miss');
    if not male and not married and not young then writeln('call her Ms');
end.
```

Try re-writing this section using an extended if ... then ... else ... structure.

41

case branching

if ... then will handle a single conditional 'detour'; if ... then ... else will handle two-way splits, but what if you have a whole bunch of alternatives? Look back to the *if calculator* (page 35). There's a better way to cope with sets of options – the **case** structure. It takes the form:

```
case variable of
    value(s) : statement;
    value(s) : statement;
    ...
else  action-if-variable-not-recognised
end;
```

Here is the same program, re-written using case.

The case calculator

```
program calc3;

var
  total, num  : real;
  op          : char;

begin
    write('Enter first number: ');
    readln(total);
    write('Enter next number: ');
    readln(num);
    repeat
        write('What sort of sum(+-*/) ');
        readln(op);
        case op of
            '+' : total := total + num;
            '-' : total := total - num;
            '*' : total := total * num;
            '/' : total := total / num;
        else writeln('Invalid response ');
        end;
        writeln('The answer is ',total:0:3);
        write('Enter next number or 0 to quit: ');
        readln(num);
    until num = 0;
end.
```

The **else** line takes care of those values that are not specified above. It is optional – though in some varieties of Pascal, the program will crash if the case variable holds a value that is not catered for.

The **case** structure is even more useful where there are several values that lead to the same action. A user-friendly menu, for example, might allow two or three ways of selecting any option.

```
writeln('Create a (N)ew file .............1');
writeln('(S)ave the file .....................2');
writeln('(O)pen and existing file......3');
writeln('(E)dit the file ....................4');
writeln('E(x)it................... .............5');
readln(choice)
```

Using **if ... then**, you get lines like this:

```
if (choice = '1') or (choice = 'N') or (choice = 'n') then...
```

With **case**, you simply list the alternatives on the left of the colons.

```
case choice of
    '1','n','N' : create_action;
    '2','s','S' : save_action;
    '3','o','O' : open_action;
    '4','e','E' : edit_action;
    '5','x','X' : exit action;
end;
```

Take note

In the case structure, as elsewhere, you can replace a single statement with a block of statements enclosed in begin ... end. e.g.

```
'5', 'x', 'X' : begin
                    write('really quit?');
                    readln(yesno);
                    if (yesno = 'y') or (yesno = 'Y')
                        then done := true;
                end;
```

The unloved goto

Pascal has a **goto** statement that is ignored by most programmers and treated with disdain by the rest. I mention mainly because it is there and you might find a use for it one day.

goto makes the flow of execution leap to another part of the program, identified by a **label**. The jump can be forwards, backwards and out of **for**, **while** or **repeat** loops. To use goto, you first declare a label at the top of the program. This label can be a name or number, and several can be declared in one line.

```
label 1, 2, exit;
var
    ...
```

The **goto** jump usually starts from an **if** or **case** line:

```
if ... then goto 1;

case .. of
'q','Q' : goto exit;
    ...
```

The target for the jump is marked by the label, followed by a colon. This can be at the beginning of a line, or on a line by itself.

```
1 : writeln('Error, invalid input');

exit :  ;
```

It is **goto**'s ability to leap all over the place – and particularly out of loops – that dismays those committed to structured programming. For ease of reading, testing and debugging, a program should be divided into separate blocks, each performing a specific task. **goto** blurs the structure and can lead to 'spaghetti' programs, where tracing the flow of execution is as hard as picking one strand out of a plateful of spaghetti.

The two programs opposite both do exactly the same thing. This first uses **goto**s to loop and to exit from the loop; the second controls the flow through a **repeat**. Which is easier to follow?

Using goto...

```
program gototest;

label looptop, exit;

var
  loop,x : integer;

begin
    loop := 1;
looptop:
    readln(x);
    writeln(x);
    if x = 99 then goto exit;
    loop := loop + 1;
    if loop < 100 then goto looptop;

    exit : writeln('Goodbye');
end.
```

... and avoiding goto

```
program nogoto:
var
    loop, x : integer;
begin
    loop := 1;
    repeat
        readln(x);
        writeln(x);
        loop := loop +1;
    until (x = 99) or (loop > 100);
    writeln('Goodbye');
end.
```

Debugging

If you have been trying out the example programs, and have typed them in exactly as given (with any necessary amendments in the opening lines to suit your system), then you will not have had any bugs. As soon as you start to write your own programs, you'll start to get them regularly! Everybody does. The only reason you shouldn't get bugs with the programs in this book is because I have already had them and debugged them.

Bugs fall into two groups: syntax errors and logic errors.

Syntax errors

Syntax errors will be picked up by the compiler during its first run through the program. They must be cured before the program can be compiled successfully. The most common of these are:

● Typing mistakes in the names of variables or procedures, or using variables that have not been declared. Usually reported as **Unknown identifier**.

● Missing punctuation – typically the semi-colon at the end of a line. Normally reported as **Missing ';'** , but can generate other reports. The error will show up on the line *after* the missing semi-colon.

● The wrong types of data items passed to procedures and functions. Usually reported as **Type mismatch**.

● The wrong number of items passed as parameters. Can produce **Missing ','** or **Missing ')'** as the compiler tries to match the arguments with the parameters.

● Unmatched **begin ... end** or **repeat ... until** pairs. Reports from these vary but include the singularly unhelpful **Error in statement** and the more useful **Unexpected end of file**.

Sometimes the compiler will not be able to work out what the error is – it will just know that your code doesn't make sense to it. However, it will tell you where to start looking. Check the reported line and the line above very carefully.

Run-time errors

These arise from failures in program design, and show up in the form of strange result or crashes when you run the program. In some cases, they only occur when variables hold a certain combination of values – these can be difficult to find and to fix. When commercial software is in its beta-test stage, it is these bugs that are being sought – and some may still slip through the testing, only turning up when the programs have been used in earnest for some time.

The only way to eliminate all run-time errors is by thorough testing.

● Check every route through a branching program, to make sure that it reaches the right places.

● Check all loops through a full range of possible values.

● Where data is to be input, try first with the sort of values that you expect people to enter, then try with ones that the program is not designed to deal with – someone is bound to enter them one day.

If you cannot see why or where an error is occurring, put **writeln**s in your code at key points.

    writeln('Into display loop. Start at = ', startval, ' end at = ', endval);

They should show where the program has reached, and the values held by relevant variables. (Add a blank **readln** if necessary, to hold the display so that you can study it.)

Debugging in Unix systems

On Unix systems, the Pascal compiler will normally produce an error report listing all the errors in the program. This can be dishearteningly long, particularly on the first attempt to compile a lengthy program. Do not be dismayed! Many apparent errors are the result of a cascade effect. When the compiler hits an error, it may be a couple of lines before it can start to understand your code again, and in the meantime it will generate error reports for the intervening lines. Go through the list, fix the obvious errors and compile again. You should be pleasantly surprised by how much the error report has shrunk.

Exercises

1   Write a program, using two nested **for** loops, to produce this display:

```
         *
        ***
       ****
      *******
     *********
    ***********
```

2   Turbo Pascal has a function **random(*range*)** which generates a random number between 0 and *range–1*. (The algorithm produces a real number between 0 and *range*, but then rounds it down.) It also has a procedure **randomize** which ensures that that the random number really is random. Miss it out and you will see why it is needed. Other versions of Pascal may or may not have a random number generator.

If you can, write a program that generates a random number between 1 and 100 then asks the user to guess. It should tell the user if the guess is too high or too low, and continue to ask for further guesses until the user gets it right.

3   With the Year 2000 problem hanging over all programmers' heads, you should work out a routine for validating dates. At the very least, this should check that the day numbers do not exceed the 31, 30 or 28 (29 each leap year) limits for the months.

4   The ASCII character set can be divided into control characters (from 0 to 31), space, digits, letters (whether upper or lower case), and symbols. Write a program that will take an input character and write a message to say what kind it is.

3 Arrays, strings and sets

Arrays

Arrays provide an easy means to handle large quantities of data. An array is a collection of variables – of any type – all with the same name, but with different identifying numbers, or *subscripts*. Think of an array as a table, or a list, with numbered rows.

Arrays are defined (in the usual **var** area) by specifying their size and type like this:

```
number : array [1 .. 5] of integer;
```

This sets up an array of 5 integers, named number[1] to number[5]. Note that there are 2 dots between the first and last number, and the numbers are enclosed in square brackets. Square brackets are also used around the subscripts when identifying an *element* in the array.

```
number[1]
number[2]
number[3]
number[4]
number[5]
```

Each element can be treated as an ordinary variable. You can, for instance, write such statements as:

```
readln(number[1]);

writeln(number[3]);

answer := number[2] * number[5];
```

But this rather defeats the object of the exercise – you might just as well have defined the variables *number1*, *number2*, *number3*, etc. The real power of arrays lies in the fact that the subscript can be a variable or calculated value. You can process a whole array of data by running it through a loop. Look at this fragment from the next program. It adds the values from all the element in the array to the total – and the code is exactly the same whether there are 5 or 5 million elements.

```
for loop := 1 to counter do

    total := total + nums[loop];
```

Simple arrays

```
program arrays1;

var
  nums :  array[1..10] of real;
  counter, loop :  integer;
  total,average : real;

begin
  writeln('This program calculates averages');

  {collect values}
  counter := 0;
  repeat
      counter := counter + 1;
      write('Enter next number or 0 to stop: ');
      readln(nums[counter]);
  until (nums[counter] = 0) or (counter = 10);

  {ignore the last}
  if nums[counter] = 0
     then counter := counter -1;

  {display array contents}
  for loop := 1 to counter do
      writeln(loop,nums[loop]:8:2);

  {calculate total and average}
  total := 0;
  for loop := 1 to counter do
     total := total + nums[loop];
  average := total / counter;
  writeln('Total = ', total:0:2);
  writeln('Data items = ',counter);
  writeln('Average = ',average:0:2);
end.
```

This can be any size, and start and end at any subscripts – as long as the end is larger than the start. The array does not have to start at 1. [0..99] is a valid size – so are [50..60] and [–100..100]. Starting at either 0 or 1 is the usual practice.

This is nums[1] first time round, then nums[2] and so on.

51

The Sieve of Erastothenes

You can use this second example of arrays to test the speed and capacity of your system.

The Sieve of Erastothenes finds prime numbers by a process of elimination. It is based on the principle that if you remove all multiples of numbers, you must be left with primes. It works like this. Take a block of numbers, start from 2 (1 does not count as a prime number) and cross out all multiples of 2.

```
1  2  3  4  5  6  7  8  9  10 11 12 13 14 15 16
      x     x     x     x     x     x     x     x
```

The next number after 2 which has not been crossed off is 3. This must be a prime as there is nothing smaller than it which can be divided into it equally. We now run through the block again, this time crossing out multiples of 3.

```
1  2  3  4  5  6  7  8  9  10 11 12 13 14 15 16
      x  ^  x     x     x  x  x     x     x  x  x
```

4 has been crossed off. It is not a prime and there is no point in crossing out its multiples as the same numbers must also be multiples of 2. 5 is the next prime. We go off through the block again, crossing out multiples of this – and nothing visible happens as the next un-crossed-off multiple of 5 is off the page at 25!

```
1  2  3  4  5  6  7  8  9  10 11 12 13 14 15 16
      x  ^  x  ^  x     x  x  x     x     x  x  x
```

With the sieve program, the block is held in the array numset. Initially all its elements are set to 0 – and note that this must be done explicitly as not all Pascals will zero arrays for you. They are changed to 1 if they are found to be a multiple.

Note the use of the constant MAX to set the size of the array (and the end of the loops). Set this to a low value when first testing the program, then push it up to find the limits of your system. These limits are not set by physical memory, but by the way your version of Pascal accesses memory.

Sieve of Erastothenes

```
program sieve;

const
    MAX = 10000;

var
 numset   : array [1..MAX] of integer;
 num      : integer;
 loop     : integer;
 count    : integer;

begin
    count := 0;

    num := 2;

    for num := 2 to MAX do
       numset[num] := 0;

    for num := 2 to MAX do
    begin
        if numset[num] = 0    {prime, not crossed out}
        then
           begin
               count := count + 1;
               write(num:6);
               loop := num + num;
               while loop <= MAX do
               begin
                   numset[loop] := 1;     {cross out multiples}
                   loop := loop + num;
               end;
           end;
    end;
    writeln;
    writeln('Total number of primes found = ',count);
end.
```

The multiplier, initialised to 2.

Set all elements to 0.

Display primes.

Start at first multiple.

Loop through in steps of 2, then 3, then 5, etc.

Array dimensions

The arrays that we have used so far have only had one dimension – a simple list of numbers. Pascal arrays can have any number of dimensions. These are all valid definitions:

```
table : array [1..10, 1..20] of integer;
book : array [1..6, 1..50, 1..40, 1..60] of char;
```

The create arrays equivalent to a table of 10 rows and 20 columns of integers, a book of 6 chapters, with 50 pages per chapter, 40 lines per page and 60 characters per line.

In practice, it gets hard to visualise structures of more than 3 or 4 dimensions – if you are ever tempted to create arrays more complex than this, think very carefully about whether you really need to!

Here is an extension of the simple total and averages program from earlier in this chapter. It handles multiple sets of data – held in the 2-dimensional array, *table* – with totals and averages for rows and columns held in 4 separate 1-dimensional arrays.

Two-dimensional arrays

```
program arrays2;

var
    table :  array[1..10, 1..10] of real;
    rows, cols, rloop, cloop :  integer;
    ctotal,caverage : array[1..10] of real;  {column summaries}
    rtotal,raverage : array[1..10] of real;  {row summaries}

begin
    writeln('This finds totals and averages for a table of data');

    write('How many rows? ');
    readln(rows);
    write('How many columns? ');
    readln(cols);
```

2-D array – could have more than 10 by 10 elements if wanted.

Get table size.

```
            for rloop := 1 to rows do
               for cloop := 1 to cols do
               begin
                 write('Value for row ',rloop,' column ',cloop);
                 readln(table[rloop,cloop]);
               end;

            for rloop := 1 to rows do
            begin
            rtotal[rloop] := 0;
               for cloop := 1 to cols do
                  rtotal[rloop] := rtotal[rloop] + table[rloop,cloop];
            raverage[rloop] := rtotal[rloop] / cols;
            end;

            for cloop := 1 to cols do
            begin
            ctotal[cloop] := 0;
               for rloop := 1 to rows do
                  ctotal[cloop] := ctotal[cloop] + table[rloop,cloop];
            caverage[cloop] := ctotal[cloop] / rows;
            end;

            writeln('              Values          Totals  Averages');
            for rloop := 1 to rows do
            begin
               write('        ');                {spaces at start}
               for cloop := 1 to cols do
                  write(table[rloop,cloop]:6:2);
                writeln(rtotal[rloop]:8:2, raverage[rloop]:8:2);
            end;
               write('Totals   ');
               for cloop := 1 to cols do
                  write(ctotal[cloop]:6:2);
               writeln;

               write('Averages');
               for cloop := 1 to cols do
                  write(caverage[cloop]:6:2);
               writeln;
         end.
```

Data input section.

Take one row at a time ...

... and add up across the columns, storing the answers in the row total array rtotal.

Total and average the columns

Adjust the layout to suit yourself.

write places the elements across the screen ...

writeln starts a new line for the next set.

55

Strings

As we noticed in *Variables and types of data* (page 10), standard Pascal does not offer a data type for storing strings of text. If you want to store more than one character at a time, you have to set up a character array. (Turbo Pascal programmers turn to page 58!)

String storage

Now, although Pascal doesn't have a string type, it does have a special sort of array for characters, marked by the keyword **packed**. The reason for it is this. We talk of the smallest item of data in a computer system as being a *byte*, but in practical terms, the smallest item of memory that can be allocated to data is a *word*. The size of a word depends upon the system, but in a 16-bit system it is usually 2 bytes; on a 32-bit system it is 4 bytes.

The definition:

```
mytext : array [1..100] of char;
```

will set up an array of 100 characters, but normally take at least 200 bytes of memory. The preferred alternative:

```
mytext : packed array [1..100] of char;
```

stores exactly the same data, but in at least half the space.

Entering strings of text

So much for storage. What about getting the data into the packed array? Unfortunately, this does not work:

```
readln(mytext);
```

The packed array is a compound structure of separate elements, and readln can only handle one thing at a time. If you want keyboard input into a packed array, it must go in one character at a time.

```
loop := 1;
repeat
    read(c);
    mytext[loop] := c;
    loop := loop + 1;
until c = chr(13);
```

This works by taking the characters in one at a time – using **read**, not **readln** (why?) – into the char variable *c*, then adding them into the packed array. It may not always work perfectly because not all computer systems generate a character 13 when the [Enter] key is pressed. Some produce character 10 (linefeed), others a character 13 and 10 combination. The solution to this is to put another read(c) after the loop to pick up the lurking character 10. Look for it in this program.

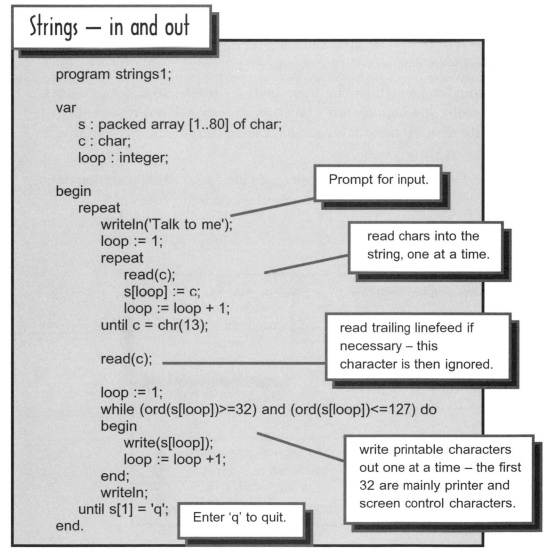

Strings — in and out

```
program strings1;

var
    s : packed array [1..80] of char;
    c : char;
    loop : integer;

begin
    repeat
        writeln('Talk to me');
        loop := 1;
        repeat
            read(c);
            s[loop] := c;
            loop := loop + 1;
        until c = chr(13);

        read(c);

        loop := 1;
        while (ord(s[loop])>=32) and (ord(s[loop])<=127) do
        begin
            write(s[loop]);
            loop := loop +1;
        end;
        writeln;
    until s[1] = 'q';
end.
```

Prompt for input.

read chars into the string, one at a time.

read trailing linefeed if necessary – this character is then ignored.

write printable characters out one at a time – the first 32 are mainly printer and screen control characters.

Enter 'q' to quit.

Turbo strings

Turbo Pascal, unlike the varieties that you may meet on Unix systems, does support string variables.

They can either be of fixed length, defined like this:

    surname : string[20];

which creates storage for a maximum of 20 characters. If anyone tries to enter overlong text into a fixed length field, the surplus will be chopped off – so *'Bertie Postlethwait-ffoulkes-Smythe'* will find his surname truncated to *'Postlethwait-ffoulke'*.

To define variable length strings, simply miss off the length:

    president : string;

Variable length strings can hold anything from 1 to 255 characters. This will cope happily with *'William Jefferson Clinton'* and just as happily with *'Al Gore'*, so you won't need to redefine the variable in four years' time!

Turbo Pascal's strings certainly make life easier. This program does exactly the same job as the one on the previous page.

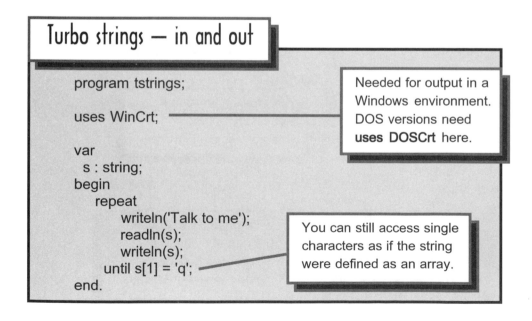

Turbo strings — in and out

```
program tstrings;

uses WinCrt;

var
  s : string;
begin
    repeat
        writeln('Talk to me');
        readln(s);
        writeln(s);
    until s[1] = 'q';
end.
```

Needed for output in a Windows environment. DOS versions need **uses DOSCrt** here.

You can still access single characters as if the string were defined as an array.

Fixed or variable length?

A typical use for fixed length fields is in record structures in databases (see page 112),but it is worth using them in any situations where you know how much space you want an item of text to take. (At machine level, variable length strings take a little more managing than do fixed length ones, though the difference in running speed should be imperceptible in most programs.)

When you write fixed length strings to the screen, unused storage at the end of the string is ignored by the system. The following program demonstrates this.

If you enter more than 10 characters, the surplus is truncated; if you enter less than 10, only those characters are displayed.

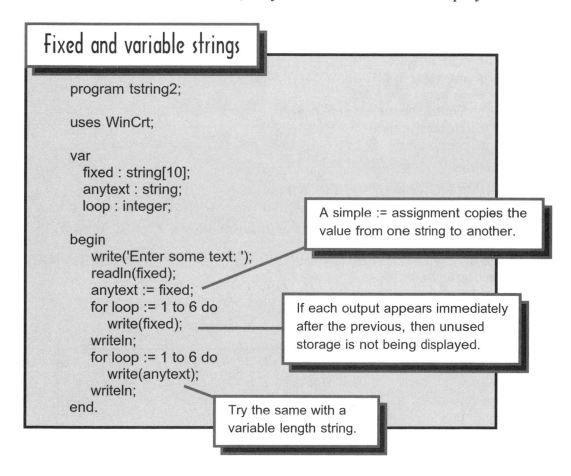

Fixed and variable strings

```
program tstring2;

uses WinCrt;

var
   fixed : string[10];
   anytext : string;
   loop : integer;

begin
   write('Enter some text: ');
   readln(fixed);
   anytext := fixed;
   for loop := 1 to 6 do
      write(fixed);
   writeln;
   for loop := 1 to 6 do
      write(anytext);
   writeln;
end.
```

A simple := assignment copies the value from one string to another.

If each output appears immediately after the previous, then unused storage is not being displayed.

Try the same with a variable length string.

Sets

Pascal allows you to take a group of values of the same type and form them into a *set*. The structure is mainly used for checking inputs to make sure that they are in an acceptable range of values.

A set is defined by enclosing the elements in square brackets. The elements may be written as individual items, separated by commas; as the start and end values of a series, separated by two dots; or by a combination of the two. These are all valid sets:

['N','n','Y','n']	acceptable answers to a Yes/No question
[0..99]	integer numbers 0 to 99
['0'..'9']	digits (numeric characters) '0' to '9'
['A'..'Z','a'..'z']	the set of all the letter characters

The first of these examples is probably one of the sets most commonly used. You will often see it in lines like this:

```
write('Would you like to exit the program (Y/N)? ');
readln(reply)
if not (reply in ['N', 'n', 'Y', 'n'])
then begin
    write('Please enter Y or N ');
    readln(reply);
    end;
```

In the line:

```
if not (reply in ['N', 'n', 'Y', 'n'])
```

the keyword **in** compares the value in *reply* with those in the set. If the value is not in the set, the user is prompted for a 'Y' or 'N' answer.

Without sets, you would need one or other of these nasty lines to check the same values:

```
if (reply <> 'N') and (reply <> 'n') and  (reply <> 'Y') and (reply <> 'y') then
```

```
if not ((reply = 'N') or (reply = 'n') or (reply = 'Y') or (reply = 'y')) then
```

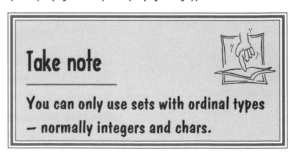

Take note

You can only use sets with ordinal types – normally integers and chars.

Simple sets

```
program settest;

var
    n : integer;
    yesno: char;

begin
    repeat
        writeln('Enter digit');
        readln(n);
        if n in [0..127] then writcln('n is between 0 and 127');
        write('Again? ');
        readln(yesno);
        while not (yesno in ['Y','y','N','n']) do
        begin
            write('Enter Y or N ');
            readln(yesno);
        end;
    until yesno in ['N','n'];
end.
```

Equivalent to:
if (n >= 0) and (n <= 127)

Must be 'Y' or 'N' —
upper or lower case.

Equivalent to:
until (yesno = 'N') or (yesno = 'n')

Tip

If you are using Turbo Pascal, take care when using sets to check number ranges. Some very large — or negative — numbers will test positive, even though they are outside the range. Low value sets are reliable, but if in doubt, use (x>...) and (x<...) tests instead.

Sets and constants

Sets can be defined into constants, at the start of a program. Definition takes the form:

constant_name = [set of values]

Here, as elsewhere, the use of constants is particularly valuable where the use of literal values would make the code hard to read, and where you need to be able to change values during later updates of the program.

This next example uses constants to classify characters into lower and upper case letters, digits and others.

Sets in constants

```
program charsets;

const
    lower = ['a'..'z'];
    upper = ['A'..'Z'];
    digit = ['0'..'9'];

var
  letter : char;

begin
    repeat
        write('Enter a character: ');
        readln(letter);
        if letter in lower
            then writeln('Lower case letter')
            else if letter in upper
                then writeln('Upper case letter')
                else if letter in digit
                    then writeln('Numeral')
                    else writeln('Symbol');
    until letter = 'q'
end.
```

Equivalent to:

if (letter >= 'a') and (letter <= 'z')

This is one multi-level **if ... then ... else** structure. **case** would have been a neater solution. Unfortunately, you cannot mix **case** and sets.

Defining types

Pascal allows you to define your own data types. At first glance you might ask, why bother? After all, data is either characters or numbers and they are well catered for. However, as you get further into the language the value of user-defined types becomes much clearer. They are crucial to string-handling in procedures (see page 86) and greatly simplify work with record structures (see page 112). They can also help with more routine chores, and add to a program's readability.

New types are defined at the top of the program – before the **const** and **var** areas. A simple type definition takes this form:

```
type
    string80 = packed array[1..80] of char;
```

After this, you have a new type, string80, which can be used to define variables:

```
var
    title : string80;
    author : string80;
    publisher:string80;
```

This is exactly the same as:

```
var
    title : packed array[1..80] of char;
    author : packed array[1..80] of char;
    publisher:packed array[1..80] of char;
```

but takes a lot less typing (no pun intended) – and the more variables you have with the same definition, the greater the advantage of using a **type** shortcut.

Take note

When we turn to the business of passing text strings to and from procedures (page 86), you will see that defining packed arrays as types is not merely convenient, but essential.

Typing sets

While most user-defined types are based on existing data types –
typically in a compound form – you can create completely new ones
using sets. To be honest, I've never found a great deal of use for this,
but that may just be my approach to programming. However, it does
lead to some intriguing code. Look at this program, for example.

```
program days;

type
    weekday = (monday,tuesday,wednesday,thursday,friday);
var
    day : weekday;
begin
    for day := monday to friday do
        writeln('Day number', ord(day));
end.
```

> **ord()** finds its place
> in the weekday set

weekday consists only of the values *monday* to *friday* and these are
held internally as the ordinal values 0 to 4 – not as text items. So, you
can run a loop through a weekday variable, find its ord() value – just
as you can of an ASCII character. You could create the same effect with
constants, like this:

```
program constdays;

const
    monday = 0;
    tuesday = 1;
    wednesday = 2;
    thursday = 3;
    friday = 4;

var
    day : integer;
begin
    for day := monday to friday do
        writeln('Day number', ord(day));
end.
```

> **day** alone would produce the same
> effect here, as it is an integer.

One thing that you cannot do with a user-defined ordinal type is use it as a subscript of an array – at least, not directly. Here's that first weekday program, extended so that it now displays the day names. These are held in an array of 5 packed arrays of char.

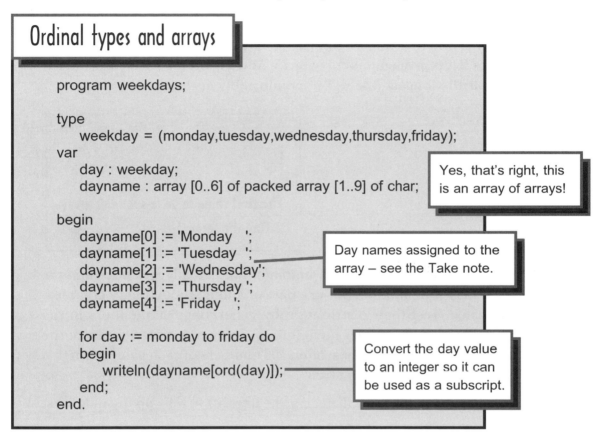

Ordinal types and arrays

```
program weekdays;

type
    weekday = (monday,tuesday,wednesday,thursday,friday);
var
    day : weekday;
    dayname : array [0..6] of packed array [1..9] of char;

begin
    dayname[0] := 'Monday   ';
    dayname[1] := 'Tuesday  ';
    dayname[2] := 'Wednesday';
    dayname[3] := 'Thursday ';
    dayname[4] := 'Friday   ';

    for day := monday to friday do
    begin
        writeln(dayname[ord(day)]);
    end;
end.
```

Yes, that's right, this is an array of arrays!

Day names assigned to the array – see the Take note.

Convert the day value to an integer so it can be used as a subscript.

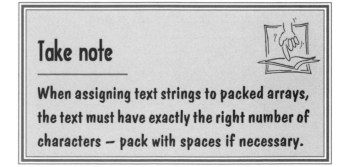

Take note

When assigning text strings to packed arrays, the text must have exactly the right number of characters – pack with spaces if necessary.

Exercises

1   Write a program that will take in a set of 10 real numbers and use them to produce a bar chart, made up of lines of asterisks across the screen. The number should be displayed at the right of the line. e.g.

      ******************** 20.4
      ********************************* 33.8

2   You will find that the program from exercise 1 produces really messy charts if it is given numbers over 75. Add a routine to scale the output so that the longest line will fit comfortably across the screen.

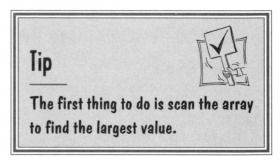

Tip

The first thing to do is scan the array to find the largest value.

3   The numbers generated by **random()** are actually *pseudo-random*. They may look random but are part of a long, though very complex, sequence. Test their distribution by generating 600 numbers in the range 1 to 6, and collect them into an array of 6 integers. Check the array at the end. If you get around 100 numbers of each value, then this is a good random distribution.

     Tip: at some point you will need a line like this to tally up the numbers:

```
numbers[x] := numbers[x] + 1;
```

4   Rewrite the first sets example (page 61) using constants.

5   Rewrite the character analysis program (exercise 2.4) using sets.

4 Structured programming

Program structure

A fully developed Pascal will consist of a number of blocks of code, each performing a particular task. We have already met some of these blocks – those enclosed in **begin ... end** or **repeat ... until**. There are also more developed types of blocks – *procedures* and *functions* – which can be viewed almost as programs within the main program.

Procedures

A procedure is a chunk of code, designed to do a specific job. This will typically involve taking in one or more values (or *parameters*) and processing them in some way. You can see this in two of the built-in procedures that we have been using regularly – **writeln** and **readln**.

> **writeln**(*values-or-variables*)

writeln takes the values or variables that are passed to it and displays them on the screen. It's a one-way process – the values and variables are not changed by the procedure.

> **readln**(*variables*)

With **readln**, you have a two-way process. The names of one or more variables are passed to it from the program. The procedure then collects values from the keyboard, and passes them back to the main program through the variables.

When you define your own procedures, they take this shape:

```
procedure  name(parameter_name:type, parameter_:type);
var
    variable_declarations
begin
    statements
end;
```

The procedure *name*, like a program name, can be any single word. There can be any number of *parameters*, each followed by its type – as invariable declarations. Note the semi-colon at the end of that line! *Variables* are optional. Any declared here can only be used within the procedure – though the variables declared at the top of the program are also available within the procedure. (See *The scope of variables*, page 82, for more on this.)

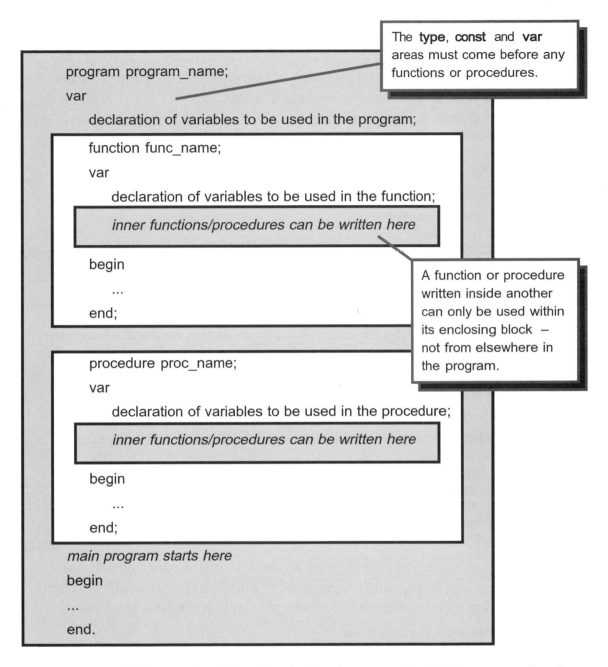

The **type**, **const** and **var** areas must come before any functions or procedures.

program program_name;

var

declaration of variables to be used in the program;

function func_name;

var

declaration of variables to be used in the function;

inner functions/procedures can be written here

begin

...

end;

A function or procedure written inside another can only be used within its enclosing block – not from elsewhere in the program.

procedure proc_name;

var

declaration of variables to be used in the procedure;

inner functions/procedures can be written here

begin

...

end;

main program starts here

begin

...

end.

This is a stylised view of a structured program. Most features are optional! There may be many functions and procedures, or none. Each part may – or may not – have its own set of variables (but see page 86). Functions and procedures can be written within other functions and procedures.

A simple procedure to display real values as currency ('£' in front, and 2 decimal places). If you had a lot of currency displays in a program, it might be worth using something like this.

```
procedure currency(n:real);
begin
    write('£',n:0:2);
end;
```

Within the program, it would be called up like this:

```
currency(cash);
```

The value in *cash*, a real variable, is passed to the parameter *n*, and then displayed by the procedure.

Functions

Functions differ from procedures in one important respect. A function always returns a value, which can be used in a calculation, passed to a variable or displayed on screen. We met some of Pascal's built-in functions earlier (*Number functions*, page 20). Now let's see how to create our own. This is the basic shape:

```
function  name(parameter_name:type, parameter:type):return_type;
var
    variable_declarations
begin
    statements
    name := return_value
end;
```

You must give the *return_type* at the end of the function line, and before you leave the function, you must pass the result to the function's name. Here is a function to calculate the cube of a number.

```
function  cube(n:real):real;
begin
    cube := n * n * n;
end;
```

In this next example you can see a simple function and procedure at work in a program.

Adding by function

```
program add3;

var
  a,b,c: integer;

function sum(x,y: integer):integer;
var
  total : integer;
begin
  total := x + y;
  sum := total;
end;

procedure display(n:integer);
begin
  writeln('The answer is ',n);
end;

{main program starts here}
begin
  write('Enter a number: ');
  readln(a);
  write('Enter another: ');
  readln(b);
  c := sum(a,b);
  display(c);
end.
```

The values of **a** and **b** in the program are passed into **x** and **y**. The calculated total is passed back through sum to the program.

Procedures

This next program is very trivial – it tells you how many days old you are – but it does demonstrate most of the essential aspects of working with procedures.

First look at the main program. It consists of these few lines:

```
begin
    writeln('Happy Birthday!');
    getage(years);
    calculate;
    display(years,days);
end.
```

All this does is control the overall flow of the program by calling up procedures – they do all the real work. This is good. It means that when someone else comes to do work on your program – or when you come back to revise it after a few months – the shape and the main flow is immediately visible.

Now let's turn to the procedures. We'll start with the simplest.

```
procedure calculate;

var
    leaps : integer;

begin
    leaps := years mod 4;
    days := years * 365 + leaps;
end;
```

There are three variables in use here. Two of them, *years* and *days*, are declared at the top of the program; *leaps* is declared within this procedure. We will come back to the scope of variables shortly (page 86), for the moment it is enough to know that **global** (program-level) variables can be accessed from within a procedure, but **local** (procedure-level) variables can only be used inside it. After a value has been assigned to days in the procedure, it will be there when flow returns to the main program.

When the program calls this procedure it does it with the simple:

```
calculate;
```

Using procedures

```pascal
program procs;

uses WinCrt;

var
  years, days : integer;

procedure calculate;

var
  leaps : integer;

begin
    leaps := years mod 4;
    days := years * 365 + leaps;
end;

procedure display(yy: integer; dd : integer);

begin
    writeln('You are ',yy ,' years or ',dd,' days old');
end;

procedure getage(var yy : integer);

begin
    write('Enter age: ');
    readln(yy);
end;

begin
    writeln('Happy Birthday!');
    getage(years);
    calculate;
    display(years,days);
end.
```

Parameters

The display procedure is an example of one where the program passes values into it. When the program calls with:

```
display(years,days)
```

The values in *years* and *days* are passed into the **parameters** *yy* and *dd* in the procedure's title line.

```
procedure display(yy: integer; dd : integer);

begin
    writeln('You are ',yy ,' years or ',dd,' days old');
end;
```

Parameter declaration takes the same basic form as ordinary variable declaration – not surprising really, as it is doing the same job of creating named storage space. *yy* and *dd* can be used within the procedure in exactly the same way as variables.

The last procedure also has a parameter, but its declaration is subtly – but significantly different.

```
procedure getage(var yy : integer);

begin
    write('Enter age: ');
    readln(yy);
end;
```

That var at the start of the declaration makes this a two-way parameter. When the program calls this up with:

```
getage(years);
```

the value in *years* is passed into *yy* on the way into the procedure, and that in *yy* is passed to *years* on the way back. (If you want to get technical, what actually happens is that the program passes the address of the years variable, and the procedure stores the new value into that address on return to the program.)

As procedures can access those variables declared in the main program, you might ask why we bother with parameters – why not simply work with the program variables? The answer is that parameters make procedures more self-sufficient and reusable.

Look at the procedure in this program:

```
program paraproc;
var
    filler : char;

procedure centreline;
var
    loop : integer;
begin
    write('                   ');
    for loop := 1 to 40 do write(filler);
    writeln;
end;

begin
    filler := '*';
    centreline;
end.
```

The procedure writes a character 40 times – centering the line by writing 20 spaces first. The character is held in *filler*, a global variable. If I wanted to reuse this procedure in another program, it must also have the same *filler* variable used for the same purpose. With a procedure as a trivial as this, and a variable name as unusual as this, that should not be a problem. In the real world, there is a real possibility of clashes in a program and imported, reused, procedures.

Now look at what happens when we use a parameter.

```
procedure centreline(filler : char);
    ...
    for loop := 1 to 40 do write(filler);
    ...
```

This can be called from the program by the line:

```
centreline('*');
```

or by the lines:

```
marker := '*';
centreline(marker)
```

The program variable that holds the character – here called *marker* – could be called anything. You could even call it *filler*, as *filler* in the procedure is a completely separate, independent entity. (See page 86 for more on this.)

If we wanted to make our *centreline* procedure even more reusable, we could add a further parameter to control the number of times the character is written:

```
procedure centreline(filler: char; howmany : integer);
var
    loop : integer;
    offset : integer;
begin
    offset := (80 - howmany) div 2;
    for loop := 1 to offset do write(' ');
    for loop := 1 to howmany do write(filler);
    writeln;
  end;
```

The code has become a little more complicated as we must now work out how far across to push the start of the fillers, but we have a much more flexible procedure. For instance, this code:

```
size := 2;
repeat
    centreline2('#',size);
    size := size + 2;
until size = 40;
```

Produces this display:

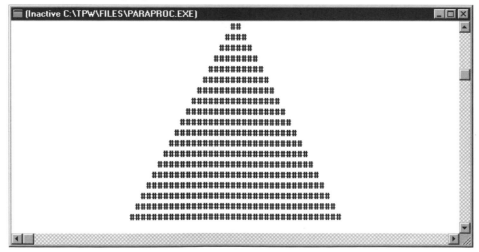

Arrays in parameters

If you want to pass an array into a procedure, you must first define the array as a type. This prevents errors arising from the variation in the sizes of the arrays in the variable and the parameter definitions.

You can see an example of this in the next program, and you will see further examples later when we turn to strings.

Arrays as parameters

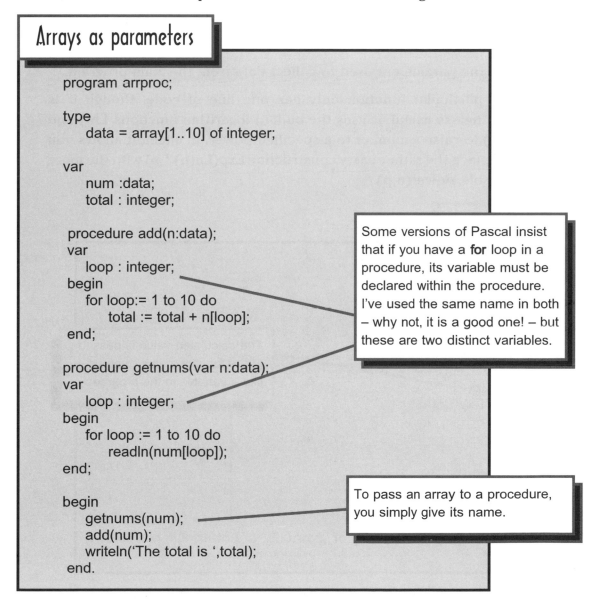

```
program arrproc;

type
    data = array[1..10] of integer;

var
    num :data;
    total : integer;

procedure add(n:data);
var
    loop : integer;
begin
    for loop:= 1 to 10 do
        total := total + n[loop];
end;

procedure getnums(var n:data);
var
    loop : integer;
begin
    for loop := 1 to 10 do
        readln(num[loop]);
end;

begin
    getnums(num);
    add(num);
    writeln('The total is ',total);
end.
```

Some versions of Pascal insist that if you have a **for** loop in a procedure, its variable must be declared within the procedure. I've used the same name in both – why not, it is a good one! – but these are two distinct variables.

To pass an array to a procedure, you simply give its name.

77

Functions

You'll recall that the only real difference between procedures and functions is that functions return a value to the main program. You can use them in any situation where you could use a literal value or a variable.

Like variables, every function has a type definition. This is written at the end of its title line, and determines the type of data returned to the program. For example, *power*, defined below, produces a real value.

```
function power(n,p  : real):real;
```

Note the parameters used to collect data from the main program.

This particular function only has one line of code, though it is nonetheless useful. It uses the built-in logarithm functions **Ln()** and **Exp()** to raise a number to a specified power. In effect, it allows you to replace the rather nasty construction **Exp(Ln(n) * p)** with the more readable **power(n,p)**.

A power function

```
program powerfunc;

var
 num, pow : real;

function power(n,p  : real):real;

begin
    power := Exp(Ln(n) * p);
end;

begin
    write('Enter number: ');
    readln(num);
    write('Enter power: ');
    readln(pow);
    writeln(num:0:2,' to the power of ',pow:0:2,' is ',power(num,pow):0:2);
end.
```

The calculated value is passed to the function name, then used like a variable in the program.

Every function must have a line in which the value that it calculates is passed to the function name. This does not just pass the value back to the calling program, it is also the exit from the function. Sometimes there will be more than one such line. The function in this program converts lower to uppercase letters and has two possible exits. The first is for converted characters, the second returns any non-lower case characters in their original state.

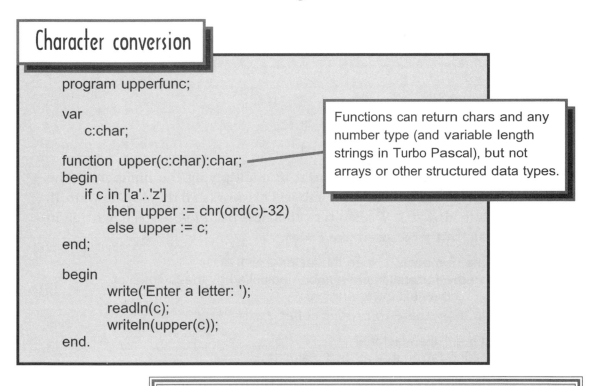

Character conversion

```
program upperfunc;

var
    c:char;

function upper(c:char):char;
begin
    if c in ['a'..'z']
        then upper := chr(ord(c)-32)
        else upper := c;
end;

begin
        write('Enter a letter: ');
        readln(c);
        writeln(upper(c));
end.
```

Functions can return chars and any number type (and variable length strings in Turbo Pascal), but not arrays or other structured data types.

Tip

Once you have got a function working properly, copy its code (just the function) into a separate file. You can then copy and paste it from here into any later programs. Turbo Pascal also has special techniques for incorporating multiple files into a program.

Recursion

Recursion is an intriguing and important technique in programming. It involves calling a function from within itself, so it is basically circular – though there must always be an escape route!

Factorials offer a good opportunity to demonstrate recursion. (For the benefit if non-mathematicians, a factorial number is a whole number that is multiplied by every other one lower than it. They are used a lot in probability calculations. A factorial is indicated by ! (shriek) after the number, e.g. 4!)

Look at the start of the factorial sequence.

        1! = 1
        2! = 2 * 1   or   2 * 1!
        3! = 3 * 2 * 1   or   3 * 2!
        4! = 4 * 3 * 2 * 1   or   4 * 3!

You can work out any factorial by multiplying the number by the factorial of the next lower number. This works all the way down to 1!, which is always 1. We can turn this into *pseudo-code* (i.e. written in English, but structured like code):

        if the number is 1, then the factorial is 1
        else the factorial is the number multiplied by the factorial of
                the next lower number.

and go from there to proper code:

```
if n = 1 then factorial := 1
    else factorial := n * factorial(n-1);
```

So, if you first call the function with the expression **factorial(3)**, it will produce the expression **3 * factorial(2)** – calling itself. On the next time round, it generates **2 * factorial(1)**, and calls itself again. This time it finds the answer 1, and returns the value to the previous call, which uses this to calculate the value **2**, returning that to the top level. At this point the function does **3 * 2**, and comes up with the answer **6** which it passes back to the program.

```
program shriek;

var
  number : real;

function factorial(n:real):real;

begin
  if n = 1 then factorial := 1
    else factorial := n * factorial(n-1);
end;

begin
    writeln('Factorial calculator.');
    write('Enter a number: ');
    readln(number);
    writeln('Factorial ',number:0:0,' = ',factorial(number):0:0);
end.
```

> Try it first with small values –
> ones that you can check easily
> yourself – then test the limits of
> your system. Mine crashes
> when the number is 34 or more.

If you want to get a clearer idea of what is happening inside the function as it cycles round, insert this line at the start:

    writeln('Entering function with value ',n:0:0);

It messes up the final output as the function's writelns insert themselves into the display. You should get something like this (input shown in **bold**):

```
Factorial calculator.
Enter a number: 4

Factorial 4 = Entering function with value 4
Entering function with value 3
Entering function with value 2
Entering function with value 1
24
```

The scope of variables

The scope of a variable means those parts of the program from which it can be accessed.

- **Global** variables – those declared at program level – can be read and changed from any part of the program.

- **Local** variables – declared in the body of the parameter list of a procedure – only exist within that procedure. When the program flow leaves the prodecure, the values in local variables are lost.

The program opposite demonstrates global and local variables. I have used the same set of variable names throughout, which is initially confusing, but it should help to emphasise the importance of *where* they are declared.

When run, the program produces output like this:

```
In main program
a = 1 b = 2 c = 3 d = 4
Calling one
In procedure one, on arrival
a = 1 b = 2 c = 19047 d = 4
In procedure one, after assignments
a = 5 b = 6 c = 7 d = 8
After procedures called
a = 1 b = 6 c = 3 d = 8
```

Notice that on entry to the procedure, **a** and **b** have the values they were passed through the parameters, and the global **d** retains its value from the program. The local **c** will have a garbage value as nothing has yet been assigned to it.

New values are assigned to all the values in the procedure. On the return to the program, **b** still has the new value (returned through the var parameter), and so does **d** (globals can be changed anywhere). **a** and **c** have reverted to their original values.

```
program scope;

var
  a,b,c,d : integer;

  procedure one(a: integer; var b:integer);

  var
    c: integer;

  begin
      writeln('In procedure one, on arrival');
      writeln('a = ',a,' b = ',b,' c = ',c,' d = ',d);
      a := 5;
      b := 6;
      c := 7;
      d := 8;
      writeln('In procedure one, after assignments');
      writeln('a = ',a,' b = ',b,' c = ',c,' d = ',d);
  end;

{main program starts here}
begin
    a := 1;
    b := 2;
    c := 3;
    d := 4;
    writeln('In main program');
    writeln('a = ',a,' b = ',b,' c = ',c,' d = ',d);
    writeln('Calling one');
    one(a,b);
    writeln('After procedures called');
    writeln('a = ',a,' b = ',b,' c = ',c,' d = ',d);
end.
```

a is a one-way parameter – any changes will not be passed back to the program.

b is a var parameter – its new value will be returned.

c is a local variable – distinct from the global variable **c**.

Try passing other variables here, instead of **a** and **b**.

Exercises

1   Rewrite the *power* function so that it uses a recursive technique to calculate the result. It should be simpler than the log-based one, working only with integer powers, and should contain an expression something like this:

```
power := n * power(n,p-1)
```

2   Drawing on the *barchart* and *average* programs of the last section, write a program to perform a range of statistical operations. It should have a menu, the **case** portion of which is shown here.

```
case choice of
    '1' :    getdata(nums);
    '2' :    barchart(nums);
    '3' :    writeln('The total is ',total(nums):0:2);
    '4' :    writeln('The average is ',average(nums):0:2);
    '5' :    writeln('The maximum is ',max(nums):0:2);
    '6' :    writeln('The minimum is ',min(nums):0:2);
    '7' : ;
else writeln('Invalid choice')
end;
```

You will see that it calls up two procedures and four functions. Whenyou are writing the *average* function, use the *total* function to sum the values.

5 Strings and numbers

Procedures for strings

Back in the last chapter, we developed a couple of routines for reading data into packed arrays and displaying them on screen. If we convert these to procedures, we can reuse them in new programs.

For maximum reusability we should use parameters for passing values into and out of the procedures. When those values are in strings or other arrays, you hit a minor snag as you cannot define a parameter directly as an array. This line produces an error report:

```
procedure stringin(s: packed array[1..80] of char);
```

The solution is to turn the array into a **type**. After

```
type
    string80 = packed array [1..80] of char;
```

you can set up the procedure with this:

```
procedure stringin(var s: string80);
```

The variable that is passed to this parameter must also be defined with the same type.

```
var
    words : string80;
```

This is essential – a matching packed array definition will not do.

Look out for the use of types in this next program. Also notice that *stringin* has *(**var** s:string80)*, while *stringout* has *(s:string80)*. The *var* allows the procedure to pass the value in *s* back to the program.

Strings in and out

```
program stringprocs;

type
    string80 = packed array [1..80] of char;

var
    words : string80;
```

```
procedure stringin(var s: string80);
var
    loop : integer;
    c    : char;

begin
    loop := 1;
    read(c);
    while (ord(c)>=32) and (ord(c)<=126) do
        begin
            s[loop] := c;
            loop := loop +1;
            read(c);
        end;
    read(c);
    s[loop] := chr(0);
end;

procedure stringout(s: string80);
var
    loop : integer;
    c    : char;

begin
    loop := 1;
    while (ord(s[loop])>=32) and (ord(s[loop])<=128) do
        begin
            write(s[loop]);
            loop := loop +1;
        end;
    writeln;
end;

begin
    repeat
        writeln('Talk to me');
        stringin(words);
        stringout(words);
    until words[1] = 'q';
end.
```

> Only accept printable characters.

> The chr(0) at the end of the string acts as a terminator. It will stop the stringout procedure running beyond the end of the entered text.

Turbo string functions

Turbo Pascal has a special set of functions and procedures for manipulating strings. The next program demonstrates these, and they are outlined below, in order of complexity.

Data can be provided to them either as literal text (in 'quotes') or as variables defined as type **string**. Where a variable must be used – to take the new string back to the program, it is marked as ***stringvar*** in this list.

integer := length(string)

Returns the number of characters in a string.

integer := pos(char, string)

Returns the position of the first occurrence of the character.

stringvar := copy(string, start,number)

Copies a *number* of characters, starting at *start*, from within a string into a second string.

stringvar := concat(string1,string2)

This concatenates two or more strings together to create a new string.

delete(stringvar,start, number)

This is a procedure – not a function. It deletes a number of characters from within the string, giving a shorter version of the same variable.

insert(new__string,base__stringvar,position)

This procedure inserts the *new_string* into the *base_string*, starting at the given *position*.

Turbo string functions

```
program tstringfuns;

var
    s1, s2, s3 : string;
    len : integer;
    position : integer;

begin
    s1 := 'Pascal';
    writeln('s1 contains ',s1);

    len := length(s1);
    writeln('s1 is ',len,' characters long');

    s2 := copy(s1,1,4);
    writeln('the first 4 characters of s1 are ',s2);

    position := pos('c',s1);
    writeln('The letter c is at ',position);

    delete(s1,4,1);
    writeln('but not any more... s1 now holds ',s1);

    insert('c',s1,4);
    writeln('and now it is back... ',s1);

    s2 := 'Made Simple';
    s3 := concat(s1,s2);
    writeln('Stick them together to make ',s3);
    s3 := concat(s1,' ',s2);
    writeln('... or include a space between the two: ',s3);

end.
```

Try different numbers here.

Try these with s1 (assigned suitable values) instead of 'c'

You often need to include a space when concatenating.

New string functions

The functions and procedures described in this section perform the same string-handling functions as the Turbo ones covered in the previous two pages. Apart from being useful – look out for them in later programs – they raised some interesting problems of design.

A few points to note about them:

● They are all designed to work with variables of *string80* type, defined by:

type
    string80 : packed array [1..80] of char;

● They are compatible with the *stringin* and *stringout* procedures developed earlier.

● They do not have the crash-proofing or the flexibility of the Turbo routines – I tried to keep them simple.

integer := length(string)

As *stringin* marks the end of its text with a **chr(0)**, we can simply search for this to find the length of the string. A while loop is used to check each character in turn, picked out of the string by the count variable. The loop stops when chr(0) is found, but as this is after the text, we must subtract 1 to find the length.

```
function length(s:string80):integer;
var
    count : integer;

begin
    count := 1;
    while s[count] <> chr(0) do
        count := count + 1;
    length := count-1;
end;
```

integer := pos(char,string)

If this function just returned the position of the character, it would be quite a lot shorter. It would simply loop through, checking each character until it found a match, and then stop. However, it also has a second job – to return 0, if no matching character is found.

This means that there are two possible exits from the search loop – either the character is found, or the end of the string is reached – and what happens next depends upon why the loop ended.

The solution I have used here is to bring in a boolean variable, *found*, which is set to **true** if a match is found. The variable is then used to control the flow around the loop and to decide whether to return the position or 0.

```
function pos(c:char; s:string80):integer;
var
 count : integer;
 found : boolean;
begin
    count := 1;
    found := false;
    while (not found) and (count <= length(s)) do
    begin
      if s[count] = c
        then found := true;
      count := count + 1;
    end;
    if found
      then pos := count - 1
      else pos := 0;
end;
```

As count is incremented after the check, we must subtract 1 to get the correct position.

Take note

This function calls the **length** function. **length** must be written higher up in the same program, or otherwise defined and linked in before **pos**, for it to work.

copy(new_stringvar, old_string, start, number)

In Turbo, this was a *function*. Here, copy is a *procedure*. We cannot implement this as a function, because the return type from function cannot be arrays – even designed as a user-defined type!

This kind of job is best designed – and explained – by means of a diagram. We'll start with the string 'Made Simple', and copy 'Sim' out of it. 'S' is the 6th character, and we are copying 3.

M	a	d	e		S	i	m	p	l	e
1	2	3	4	5	6	7	8	9	10	11

S	i	m
1	2	3

We need to copy characters 6 (the start value) to 8 from the old string into places 1 to 3 (the number to copy) in the new string. The simplest solution is to run the new string through a **for** loop of **1 to number**, while moving the **start** value along the old string.

```
procedure copy(var news:string80; olds:string80; start:integer; num:integer);
var
    loop : integer;

begin
    for loop := 1 to num do
        begin
            news[loop] := olds[start];
            start := start + 1;
        end;
    news[loop+1] := chr(0);
end;
```

> Notice the var. This first parameter passes the value back to the program.

concat(newstring, string1, string2)

This Turbo function has been implemented as a procedure, and for the same reason as before – we need to get a string value back. It is also more limited than the Turbo function in that it can only concatenate two strings at a time – the Turbo function can handle any number.

Though fairly lengthy, it is actually very simple. It loops through the first of the old strings, copying characters into the new string, tracking their positions in *count*. It then loops through the second string, still adding 1 to *count* each time, so that the second string's text is added to the first.

Note that *length* is used to find the number of characters in each string. For *concat* to work, the *length* function must therefore be present in the code, before this procedure.

```
procedure concat(var s1: string80; s2:string80; s3:string80);
var
    count : integer;
    loop : integer;

begin
    count := 1;
    for loop := 1 to length(s2) do
        begin
            s1[count] := s2[loop];
            count := count + 1;
        end;
    for loop := 1 to length(s3) do
        begin
            s1[count] := s3[loop];
            count := count + 1;
        end;
    s1[count] := chr(0);
end;
```

Tip

When trying out these procedures and functions, it may be simpler to build them all into one program, adding a little code at the bottom to set up values, call the procedures and display the results.

delete(stringvar,start,number)

There are several ways that you can tackle this job. The technique used here copies the end of the string back over the unwanted characters. For example, if we were turning 'Made It Simple' into 'Made Simple' – delete('Made It Simple', 6, 3) – moving 'Simple' back over 3 places will have the desired effect.

A diagram will help to clarify the process – and the arithmetic behind the values:

M	a	d	e		I	t		S	i	m	p	l	e
1	2	3	4	5	6	7	8	9	10	11	12	13	14

We need to move all the characters from place 9 to the end, back 3 places. 9 is 6 + 3 (*start + number*), and 3 is the number of deletions. The line that moves characters number places back is:

    s[loop-number] := s[loop];

One last little tweak. We must put a chr(0) after the text to mark its end. Once we leave the loop, *loop-number* will point to this place.

```
procedure delete(var s:string80; start:integer; number:integer);
var
    loop: integer;

begin
    for loop:= start + number to length(s) do
        s[loop-number] := s[loop];
    s[loop-number] := chr(0);
end;
```

insert(new__string;base__ stringvar; place)

We could tackle this as a sort of reverse of the *delete* procedure, shuffling characters up and dropping the new ones into place, but that could be a bit long-winded. It would need at least two, and possibly three loops, with some resetting of values in between. We can get a neater solution by to using our *copy* and *concat* procedures.

Take the situation created by these lines:

```
s1 := 'Made Simple';
insert(' Very',s1,5);
```

With copy we can chop of the first part of the string, up to the insertion point. The number of characters to be copied will be 1 less than the *place* value.

```
copy(front,s1,1,place-1);
```

front now holds 'Made' – the first 4 characters of the string.

We can copy the back half likewise. The number of characters is the length of the string – the place value + 1. Here the original string was 11 characters long, and we want the last 7. 11 - 5 + 1 = 7.

```
number := length(s1) - place + 1;
copy(back,s1,place, number);
```

And that gives us ' Simple' in *back*.

It is now a simple matter to concatenate *front* to *newbit*, and the combined string with *back*.

```
procedure insert(newbit:string80; var s1: string80; place:integer);

var
    front : string80;
    back  : string80;
    temp : string80;
    number : integer;

begin
    copy(front,s1,1,place-1);
    number := length(s1) - place + 1;
    copy(back,s1,place, number);
    concat(temp,front,newbit);
    concat(s1,temp,back);
end;
```

copy and **concat** must be defined further up the program code for this to work!

Comparing strings

In Turbo Pascal, comparing strings is no problem. In standard Pascal there is a problem, as you cannot compare arrays. The solution is to write a function to do the job for you.

The code for this is straightforward. It loops through both strings in tandem until it finds two characters that are different, or reaches the end of the shortest string. We could do this with the line:

```
while (s1[loop] = s2[loop]) and (loop <= length(s1)) and (loop <= length(s2) do
```

That is not a nice line! A neater solution is to find the length of the shortest string first:

```
        if length(s1) < length(s2)
            then size := length(s1)
            else size := length(s2);
```

That allows us to use the clearer control line:

```
        while (s1[loop] = s2[loop]) and (loop <= size) do
```

The return value is then determined by comparing the characters at the *loop* position, and is 1 if *s1* is more than *s2*, −1 if it is less and 0 if the two are the same.

```
        if s1[loop] > s2[loop]
            then strcomp := 1
            else if s1[loop] < s2[loop]
                then strcomp := -1
                else strcomp := 0;
```

This works even when the end of a string has been reached, as the next character in the shorter string will be 0, the terminator, and this is bound to be less than anything in the other string.

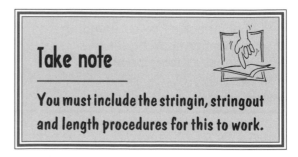

Take note

You must include the stringin, stringout and length procedures for this to work.

96

String comparison

```pascal
program stringcomp;

type
   string80 = packed array [1..80] of char;

var
  words1 : string80;
  words2 : string80;
  ans : integer;

{include procedure stringout , stringin, length}

function  strcomp(s1,s2:string80):integer;
var
   loop : integer;
   size : integer;

begin
    if length(s1) < length(s2)
        then size := length(s1)
        else size := length(s2);

    loop := 1;
    while (s1[loop] = s2[loop]) and (loop <= size) do
        loop := loop + 1;

    if s1[loop] > s2[loop]
        then strcomp := 1
        else if s1[loop] < s2[loop]
            then strcomp := -1
            else strcomp := 0;
end;

begin
        writeln('Enter first item: ');
        stringin(words1);
        writeln('Enter next item: ');
        stringin(words2);
        ans := strcomp(words1,words2);
        if ans = 1 then writeln('First larger')
        else if ans = 0 then writeln('Equal')
            else writeln('Second larger');
end.
```

FInd the shortest string and set **size** to this value.

Loop through them both.

Compare the characters at the end of the loop.

Safe number entry

As you have no doubt noticed, Pascal programs crash if you enter text where a number is expected. There are two solutions to this: train your users to be very careful, or crash-proof your number inputs. The second is easier to implement – even if you have to write your own code to do the job.

Turbo Pascal has a **Val()** function that will convert a string to an integer. For those not using Turbo – and for interested Turbo users – here is a function, *getint*, that will do the same job.

The conversion is based on these two facts.

1   The digits '0' to '9' have ASCII codes that run in series from 48 to 57. If you find the ASCII code of a digit and subtract 48, you have its numeric value:

ord('2') - 48 = 50 - 48 = 2

2   The true value of a numeral depends upon its position in the whole number. As you move left through a number, each numeral is worth 10 times more. e.g. in 123

```
3 = 3 * 1          =    3
2 = 2 * 10         =    20
1 = 1 * 10 * 10    =    100
```

The function's design is as follows:

```
go through the string from left to right until you run out of digits
    convert the current digit to a number value
    multiply the existing total by 10
    add the current number to it.
```

e.g. if the function was given the string '456'

loop	total	digit	number value	new total
1	0	'4'	4	0+4 = 4
2	4	'5'	5	40 + 5 = 45
3	45	'6'	6	450 + 6 = 456

When you have got the function working in its test program, cut it out and save it as a separate file. You can then easily copy it from there and paste it into later programs as needed.

Safe integer input

```
program intfunc;
type
    string80 = packed array[1..80] of char;
var
    strnum : string80;
    number : integer;

function getint(s : string80):integer;
var
    loop : integer;
    total : integer;
    c    : char;
    cval : integer;
begin
    total := 0;
    loop := 1;
    c := s[loop];
    while (c >='0') and (c <= '9')  do
        begin
            cval := ord(c) - 48;
            total := total * 10 + cval;
            loop := loop + 1;
            c := s[loop];
        end;
    getint := temp;
end;

begin
    write('Enter a number: ');
    stringin(strnum);
    number := getint(strnum);
    writeln('Its value is ',number);
end.
```

These can be run into one line:

total := total * 10 + ord(c) - 48

Take note

getint works in conjunction with the **stringin** procedure, so you will need to paste a copy of that into the program.

Get real!

The *getreal* function developed here is a natural development of *getint*. It also provides an opportunity to design a routine.

Let's start by looking closely at a real number.

123.4567

To the left of the decimal place, is the integer part of the number. We can use the *getint* routine to extract this part from the string.

To the right of the number is the fraction. Here the value of the digits decline by a factor of 10 as you move further right. We could design this part of the routine almost as the inverse of *getint*, dividing successive digits by 10, then 100, then 1000 before adding them in.

But before we rush into that, are there any other approaches? How about this. 123.4567 could be expressed as:

1234567 / 10000

(10000 because there are 4 decimal places, and 10000 = 10*10*10*10.) We can use the *getint* approach right through the string to get the value 1234567, and count the number of decimal places to find out how many 10's to divide it by. That could provide a simpler solution – and it's the one used here!

Minor problem. How do you count decimal places? If you were doing it 'by hand' you would look for the decimal point, then count the digits to the right. We can do the same. The variable decimal is initially set to -1, and ignored as long as it is still −1. However, when the decimal point is spotted...

```
if c = '.' then decimal := 0;
```

it brings the variable into play. On subsequent runs around the loop, it is incremented, producing the count of decimal places.

```
if decimal > -1 then decimal := decimal + 1;
```

At the end of the routine, *temp* is divided by 10 as many times as there are decimal places.

```
if decimal > 0 then
    for loop := 1 to decimal do
        temp := temp / 10;
```

The getreal function

```
function getreal(s : string80):real;
var
    loop : integer;
    temp : real;
    c    : char;
    cval : integer;
    decimal : integer;

begin
    temp := 0;
    loop := 1;
    decimal := -1;
    c := s[loop];
    while (c >='0') and (c <= '9') or (c = '.') do
        begin
            if decimal > -1 then decimal := decimal + 1;
            if c = '.' then decimal := 0;
            if (c >='0') and (c <= '9')
                then temp := temp * 10 + ord(c) - 48;
            loop := loop + 1;
            c := s[loop];
        end;
    if decimal > 0 then
        for loop := 1 to decimal do
            temp := temp / 10;
    getreal := temp;
end;
```

> If you are basing this on a copy of getint, change the function and temp from integer to real.

> if ... then statements can be written on a single line

> ... or broken up over two or more. Readability is the only thing that matters.

Take note

This is only a function. To see it in action, you will have to embed it in a test program — and don't forget to include **stringin** if necessary.

Exercises

1   Write the procedures which will copy a given number of characters from the left and right ends of a string into a new string. If you are using *stringin* and *stringout* to read and write strings, the new procedures should be compatible with them.

2   Write a procedure that will convert a string to upper case. It should call the *upper* function (page 79) to convert individual characters within the string.

3   Names are generally written with an initial capital letter, with the rest in lower case. Write a procedure that will ensure that names are converted to this format, no matter what combination of upper and lower case is used in the original string.

4   Using *getint* as the basis, write a function to take in a hexadecimal number and return its denary (base 10) value. This table may help:

Hex digit	0	1	2	3	4	5	6	7	8	9	A	B	C	D	E	F
ASCII code	48	49	50	51	52	53	54	55	56	57	65	66	67	68	69	70
Denary	0	1	2	3	4	5	6	7	8	9	10	11	12	13	14	15

In hexadecimal conversion, you must multiply by 16 as you work through the string.

$$25_{HEX} = 2 * 16 + 5 = 37_{10}$$

6 Records and files

Simple files

So far, any data that we have entered into a program has been lost as soon as the program has ended. That's fine for testing ideas and techniques, but for most real-world jobs you need to hang on to your data – and that means getting it onto a disk, and back off again later.

file variables

To access a file on a disk, you must declare a variable of type **file**. This will be used to create the link to the disk file, and to hold data in transit between the program and the disk. As part of the declaration, you must specify what type of data is to be stored in the file.

```
var
    datafile : file of integer;
```

datafile can manage the link to a file of **integer** values. You could equally well have a file of **real**, **packed array of char**, or any other type. Probably the most common data type used in filing is **record** – a compound structure that we will get to shortly.

There is also a special file type – **text** – which is mainly used for producing files that will later be printed. (Though programs can read data back in from text files if required.) These are declared like this:

```
printout : text;
```

Opening a file

There are three procedures for opening files, matching the three ways in which files are used.

rewrite   creates a new file on the disk – and if there is already one with the same name, it will be overwritten by the new one.

reset   opens an existing file for reading data from or writing it to the disk.

append   opens an existing file, so that data can be added at the end.

Turbo and standard Pascal take slightly different approaches to opening files.

Turbo opening

In Turbo, there is an assign procedure which you must use to make the initial link between the file variable and the disk file. It takes the form:

```
assign(datafile, 'dataset.dat');
```

What you call your disk files is entirely up to you, as long as the names conform to the conventions of your system. I find it convenient to give them a '.dat' or '.dta' extension to remind me that they are data files.

You then use one of the opening procedures, giving it the file variable.

```
rewrite(datafile);
reset(datafile);
append(datafile);
```

Look for the *assign* + *rewrite/reset* combinations in the next program.

Standard openings

Standard Pascal has no *assign* procedure, and makes the link between the file variable and the disk file within the opening procedure:

```
rewrite(datafilec,'dataset.dat');
reset(datafile,'dataset.dat');
append(datafile,'dataset.dat');
```

Once the files are open, standard and Turbo Pascal access them in the same way.

Transferring data to and from disk

read and **write** can be redirected to the disk, instead of the screen or keyboard, by giving the file variable as the first parameter.

```
write(datafile,num);
```

sends the contents of *num* to the *datafile*.

```
read(datafile,num);
```

takes data from the datafile and stores it in *num*.

Two points to notice here:

● You must normally use **write. writeln** can only be used with files declared as **text**.

● The data being written or read must be the same type as the file.

Closing the file

When you have finished with a file, the link to the disk must be shut down with the **close** procedure.

```
close(datafile)
```

I have talked about 'writing to disk', but in fact the data is not sent directly to the disk. It is stored initially in a buffer (temporary memory storage allocated by the system), and transferred from there when the buffer is full, or *when the file is closed*. This is important. If you do not close a file, then any data lurking in the buffer will be lost when the program ends.

Even when reading from, rather than writing to, the disk, you should close the file once you have finished with it.

Types of files

Dats can be stored in two kinds of files. The differences betwen them are mainly in how they are used – all are set up in much the same way and have the same kind of links between the disk and the program.

In *sequential* files, data is stored and accessed from the top down. When the file is opened, only the first item of data is accessible. If you want to get to, say, the fortieth item, you have to read through the intervening thirty-nine. Typically, when working with sequential files, you will read all the data into an array at the start of the program, process the data within the array, then write it all back out to disk at the end. This combination of disk file for long-term storage and arrays for immediate access is very effective, but cannot be used for large files. Pascal can only access a limited amount of memory for variable storage – Turbo Pascal on my 32Mb system, for example, has only around 48kb available for storage.

In *random access* files, you can move to any given item in the disk file and read or write it directly. This takes a little more work, but does away with the need for an array – and thus escapes the limitations of memory. The only limitation on size is disk space.

Files and arrays

This next program is an example of a sequential file, used in conjunction with an array. It has a very restricted menu – you can enter numbers into the array, display what's in it, and exit. The important work is done by the procedures *load*, at the start, and *save*, at the end, which manage the transfer between the array and the disk file.

The *save* routine is very simple – it is just a matter of opening the file, looping round to copy data from the array, and closing afterwards. (*count* is the next empty slot – one more than the number of items.)

```
begin
    assign(datafile,'nums.dta');
    rewrite(datafile);
    for loop := 1 to count - 1 do
        write(datafile,list[loop]);
    close(datafile);
end;
```

load opens and closes the file in much the same way, but has a different loop control. Look at the *while* line of this section.

```
begin
    assign(datafile,'nums.dta');
    reset(datafile);
    while not eof(datafile) do
    begin
        read(datafile,list[count]);
        count := count + 1;
    end;
    close(datafile);
end;
```

Until we have read the file in, we don't know how many items there are. Fortunately, we do not need to know. The **eof()** function checks for the End Of File, returning a true value when it is reached. We can simply set the loop to read its way through to the end of the file, copying values into the array and increment *count* as it goes. After this, *count* is pointing to the next empty slot in the array.

```
program file1;

var
    list : array[1..20] of integer;
    count: integer;
    datafile: file of integer;
    choice : char;

procedure load;
begin
    assign(datafile,'nums.dta');
    reset(datafile);
    while not eof(datafile) do
    begin
        read(datafile,list[count]);
        count := count + 1;
    end;
    close(datafile);
end;

procedure save;
var
    loop : integer;

begin
    assign(datafile,'nums.dta');
    rewrite(datafile);
    for loop := 1 to count - 1 do
        write(datafile,list[loop]);
    close(datafile);
end;

procedure getitem;

begin
    write('Data: ');
    readln(list[count]);
    count := count + 1;
end;
```

On standard systems, replace these two lines with:

reset(datfile,'nums.dta');

Checks for eof – End Of File

On standard systems, replace these two lines with:

rewrite(datfile,'nums.dta');

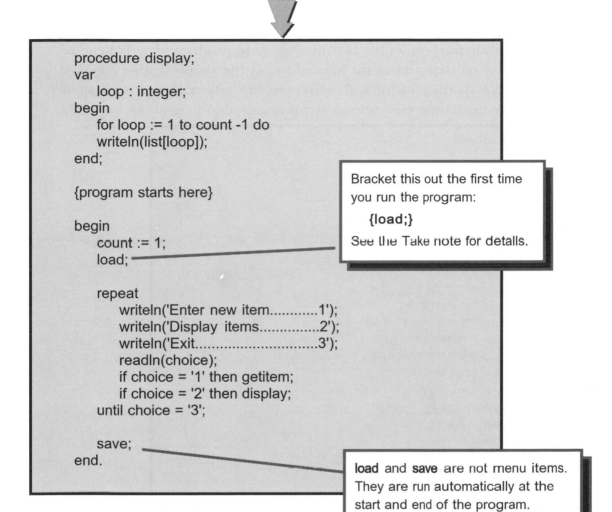

```
procedure display;
var
    loop : integer;
begin
    for loop := 1 to count -1 do
    writeln(list[loop]);
end;

{program starts here}

begin
    count := 1;
    load;

    repeat
        writeln('Enter new item............1');
        writeln('Display items..............2');
        writeln('Exit...........................3');
        readln(choice);
        if choice = '1' then getitem;
        if choice = '2' then display;
    until choice = '3';

    save;
end.
```

Bracket this out the first time
you run the program:
    {load;}
See the Take note for details.

load and **save** are not menu items.
They are run automatically at the
start and end of the program.

Take note

If you type in and run this program as given here IT WILL CRASH when it
reaches load because there will be no file for it to open. Put curly
brackets around load and run it once, so that the file is created. Now
remove the brackets from load, run again, and all should be well.

Text files

The main purpose of the **text** file type is to produce files that can be passed on to a printer for hard copy. At the simplest, this may just involve opening the file and redirecting the output. Here, for instance, is our Christmas tree screen display, amended to produce cards!

```
program xmastree;
var
 tree: text;
begin
    assign(tree,'tree.pic');
    rewrite(tree);
    writeln;
    writeln(tree,'*':40);
    writeln(tree,'***':41);
    writeln(tree,'*****':42);
    writeln(tree,'*******':43);
    writeln(tree,'*********':44);
    writeln(tree,'***********':45);
    writeln(tree,'*************':46);
    writeln(tree,'| |':41);
    writeln(tree,'-----':42);
    writeln(tree,'\   /':42);
    writeln(tree,'\_/':41);
    writeln(tree,' ');
    writeln(tree,'Happy Christmas':47);
    close(tree);
end.
```

Its output is shown here, as viewed in Notepad.

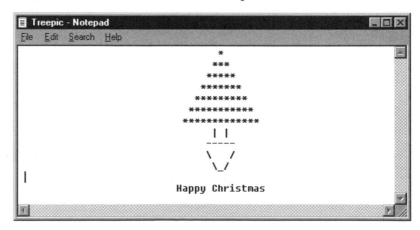

Use this next program to explore storing data in text files. It is given here in its Turbo version, using a **string** variable. If you are using a different version of Pascal, try it first with **integer** and **real** variables. The main limitation is what your system will allow you to **write** on screen – because anything that can be **writeln**'d to screen can be sent to a text file. If necessary, you may have to design a variation on the stringout procedure to write a packed array to file.

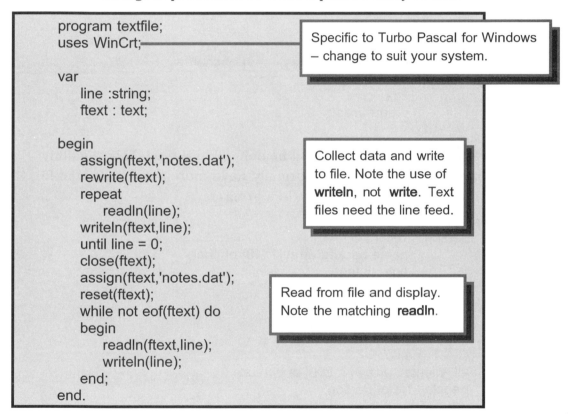

```
program textfile;
uses WinCrt;
```
Specific to Turbo Pascal for Windows – change to suit your system.

```
var
    line :string;
    ftext : text;

begin
    assign(ftext,'notes.dat');
    rewrite(ftext);
    repeat
        readln(line);
    writeln(ftext,line);
    until line = 0;
    close(ftext);
    assign(ftext,'notes.dat');
    reset(ftext);
    while not eof(ftext) do
    begin
        readln(ftext,line);
        writeln(line);
    end;
end.
```
Collect data and write to file. Note the use of **writeln**, not **write**. Text files need the line feed.

Read from file and display. Note the matching **readln**.

If you open the file in a word processor, you should get something like this – though with your text!

Notes on text files
If writing strings, the version must be able to use writeln with strings.
Any other kind of variable can be written, so text acts like any other file
The output file should be free of non-printable characters.
X

Records

A record is a compound structure, containing several fields of data, which may be of different types. Think of a record card – the sort used in a card index system. It might have on it a person's name, address, age, sex, and credit limit. Each item on the card can be read or written separately, but the whole card can be treated as one object. Pascal records are exactly the same.

You can set up a record like this:

```
var
    person : record
                name:packed array[1..40] of char;
                age : integer;
                sex : char;
                credit : real;
        end;
```

More commonly, the record will be defined as a type. This is mainly for convenience as you will normally have more than one variable with the same record structure in a program.

```
type
    person = record
                name:packed array[1..40] of char;
                age : integer;
                sex : char;
                credit : real;
        end;
var
    client : person;
    all_clients : array [1..200] of person;
    people : file of person;
```

After these declarations:

client can hold the data for one *person* record;

all_clients is an array of 200 *person* records;

people is a disk file, for data structured as *person* records.

The individual fields can be accessed in the form *recvar.field*. e.g.

```
writeln(client.age);
```

Where there are arrays, you must get the subscripts in the right place.

```
readln(all_clients[loop].sex);
if client.name[1] = 'A' then...
```

Where the record variable is an array, the subscript is linked to the main variable name; where the field is an array, the subscript goes with the field name. These are as you would expect, but it is all too easy to get the subscripts in the wrong place.

Where you have to access all the fields of a record in one block of code, for example when displaying them on screen, there is a useful shortcut that you should know about.

```
with all_clients[loop] do
    begin writeln('Client number : ',loop)
        writeln(name);
        writeln(age);
        writeln(sex);
        writeln(credit);
    end;
```

The **with *record_name* do** construction adds the *record_name* to the start of the variable names – where appropriate. In this example, *loop* is not part of the record. This will continue to be treated as *loop*. However, *name* will be treated as if it were *all_clients[loop].name*, and the other fields will likewise have the record name attached.

The whole contents of one record variable can be copied to another of the same type in a single operation:

```
all_clients[loop] := client;
write(people,client)
```

Look at that last example line again. A single **write** sends all the fields of a record (*client*) to a file (*people*). (Though each field needs a separate **write** or **writeln** to send it to the screen.)

The following program will store and display details of your CD collection. It uses the same file and array approach of the example on page 108, but with records instead of simple variables.

Records — and CDs!

```pascal
program records1;

uses WinCrt;

type
    cd = record
        artist:string[40];
        title :string[40];
        style :char;
    end;

var
    collection: array[1..50] of CD;
    diskfile : file of CD;
    counter : integer;
    choice  : char;

procedure save;
var
    loop : integer;
begin
    assign(diskfile,'cd.dta');
    rewrite(diskfile);
    for loop := 1 to counter-1 do
        write(diskfile,collection[loop]);
    close(diskfile)
end;

procedure load;
begin
    assign(diskfile,'cd.dta');
    reset(diskfile);
    while not eof(diskfile) do
    begin
        read(diskfile,collection[counter]);
        counter := counter + 1;
    end;
end;
```

Specific to Turbo Pascal for Windows – change to suit your system.

Replace if necessary with **packed array [1..40] of char**

The array and the file have matching record structures.

for loop variables must be declared in their procedures

save and **load** are essentially the same as in the earlier *files and arrays* program.

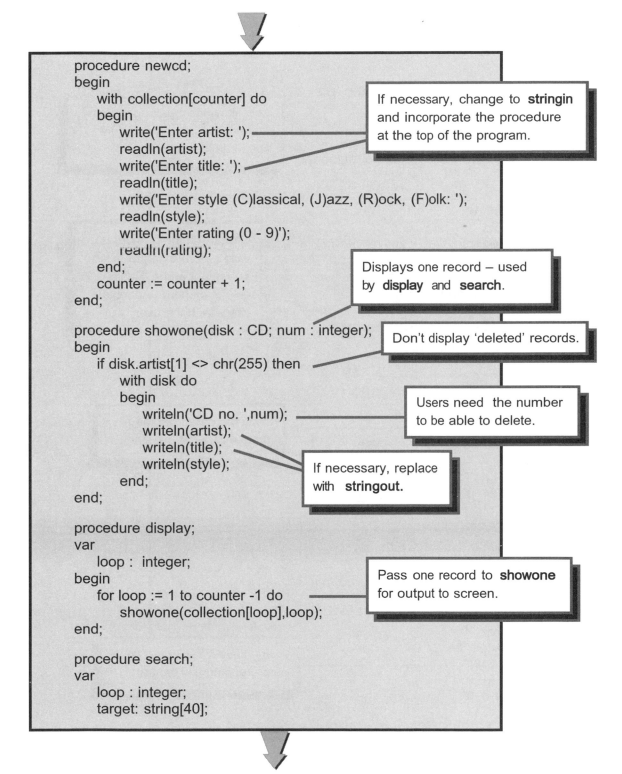

```pascal
procedure newcd;
begin
    with collection[counter] do
    begin
        write('Enter artist: ');
        readln(artist);
        write('Enter title: ');
        readln(title);
        write('Enter style (C)lassical, (J)azz, (R)ock, (F)olk: ');
        readln(style);
        write('Enter rating (0 - 9)');
        readln(rating);
    end;
    counter := counter + 1;
end;

procedure showone(disk : CD; num : integer);
begin
    if disk.artist[1] <> chr(255) then
        with disk do
        begin
            writeln('CD no. ',num);
            writeln(artist);
            writeln(title);
            writeln(style);
        end;
end;

procedure display;
var
    loop : integer;
begin
    for loop := 1 to counter -1 do
        showone(collection[loop],loop);
end;

procedure search;
var
    loop : integer;
    target: string[40];
```

Annotations:

- If necessary, change to **stringin** and incorporate the procedure at the top of the program.
- Displays one record – used by **display** and **search**.
- Don't display 'deleted' records.
- Users need the number to be able to delete.
- If necessary, replace with **stringout**.
- Pass one record to **showone** for output to screen.

115

```
begin
    writeln('Enter artist to search for: ');
    readln(target);
    for loop := 1 to counter do
        if collection[loop].artist = target
        then showone(collection[loop],loop);
end;

procedure delete;
var
    target : integer;
    reply  : char;
begin
    write('Record number? ');
    readln(target);
    if (target >0) and (target < counter)
        then collection[target].artist[1] := chr(255);
end;

begin
    counter := 1;
    load;
    writeln('CD collection organiser');
repeat
    writeln('New CD................1');
    writeln('Display collection....2');
    writeln('Select by artist......3');
    writeln('Delete record.........4');
    writeln('Exit..................5');
    readln(choice);
    case choice of
    '1' :    newcd;
    '2' :    display;
    '3' :    search;
    '4' :    delete;
    '5' :    save;
    end;
until choice = '5';
end.
```

> Use **showone** again for display – making this into a procedure saved quite a bit of typing!

> Check that the number is valid before trying to delete. You might add a 'Really delete' bit here to double check with the user.

> Copy the data from the file into the array at the start...

> ... and save it back onto disk before ending the program.

Deleting records

The *delete* procedure in this program does not actually remove a record from the array. Instead it places a special character at the start of the artist's name, to mark it to be ignored. This approach is quite common in data handling as it makes it possible to restore records that were deleted by mistake. (Data is precious and not to be discarded lightly.) Where deletions are rare, the scattering of 'holes' that develops over time is a small price to pay.

Where there is a higher turnover of data, unwanted records should be removed completely to save space. The **fulldelete** procedure given below does the job. It deletes records by moving back up one place all those further along in the array, then subtracting one from the *counter*. Notice how it copies the whole of one record into another with a single assignment:

```
collection[loop] := collection[loop+1];
```

Incorporate this into the program, either replacing the existing delete, or making this into another menu item.

```
procedure fulldelete;

var
    target : integer;
    loop   : integer;

begin
    write('Record number? ');
    readln(target);
    if (target >0) and (target < counter)
        then begin
            for loop := target to counter -1 do
                collection[loop] := collection[loop+1];
            counter := counter -1;
            end;
end;
```

Sorting

When you are working with large quantities of data, you need to be able to sort it into order. There are a number of different ways to sort data in an array (and in random access files), and as a general rule, the more efficient the sort, the more difficult it is to understand! In this section we will look at two of the simpler approaches.

Bubble sorts

These are the simplest to write, but are not really suitable for very large quantities of data as they are rather slow. The basis of a bubble sort is to check through the set of data, one pair of adjacent items at a time, swapping them over if they are out of order. The set is checked through again and again until no more swaps need doing. If this sounds as if it involves a lot of swapping, that's because it does. Look what happens when we sort this small set of words.

▶ indicates the pair being compared

↕ indicates a swap has been done

First run through

At Start				At end	
▶ dog ↕	cat		cat	cat	
▶ cat	▶ dog ↕		bee	bee	
bee	▶ bee	▶ dog ↕	ant	ant	
ant	ant	▶ ant	dog	3 tests, 3 swaps	

Second run through

At Start				At end	
▶ cat ↕	bee		bee	bee	
▶ bee	▶ cat ↕		ant	ant	
ant	▶ ant	▶ cat	cat		
dog	dog	▶ dog	dog	3 tests, 2 swaps	

On the third, and final run through, bee and ant will be swapped, giving a total of 9 comparison tests and 6 swaps.

There is an implementation of this sort routine in the next program. Notice how making a separate procedure out of the code that does the swapping helps to keep the sorting code clearer. This clarity become more important with more complex sorts.

The bubble sort

```
program bsort;
const
    MAX = 10;
type
    arraytype = integer;
    numlist = array[1..MAX] of arraytype;
var
    nums : numlist;
    loop : integer;
procedure swap (var a,b: arraytype);
var
    temp : arraytype;
begin
    temp := a;
    a := b;
    b := temp;
end;
procedure bubble(var list:numlist);
var
    pass : integer;
    loop : integer;
begin
    for pass := 1 to MAX-1 do
        for loop := 1 to MAX - 1 do
            if list[loop] > list[loop+1]
                then swap(list[loop],list[loop+1]);
end;
begin
    for loop := 1 to MAX do
        begin
            write('Enter data for item ',loop,': ');
            readln(nums[loop]);
        end;
    bubble(nums);
    writeln('Sorted');
    for loop := 1 to MAX do
        writeln(nums[loop]);
end.
```

The routine works equally well with any simple type of data (not records) – just change the type here to try.

The use of **arraytype** ensures that all the relevant variables are of the same type.

This is the simplest and crudest form of bubble. It can be improved – see the next page.

With packed arrays you may need to use the **stringin** and **stringout** procedures here.

The better bubble

The basic bubble sort runs through the array, checking each adjacent pair of items, one less time than there are items in the array. So, if you had 1001 items, it would perform 1000 * 1000 checks – 1,000,000! This takes time, and is partly unnecessary. With a couple of small tweaks, we can make significant improvements to the basic bubble sort.

With this sort routine, items that are moving upwards travel only one step at a time, but the one that should be at the bottom gets there on the first run through. This fact allows us to stop the checking and swapping one place higher each time round.

The example was a "worst case" – it started off upside down. In practice, most lists are already partially sorted, and it is mainly a matter of shuffling a few new items into place. Once they have been moved, the array is sorted. What we want here is something to show that no more swaps are needed. If we have a flag that we set when a swap is done, then if we reach the end of a loop and the flag is not set, we will know the list is in order, and we can stop.

Here's the better bubble. Fit it into the last program in place of **bubble**.

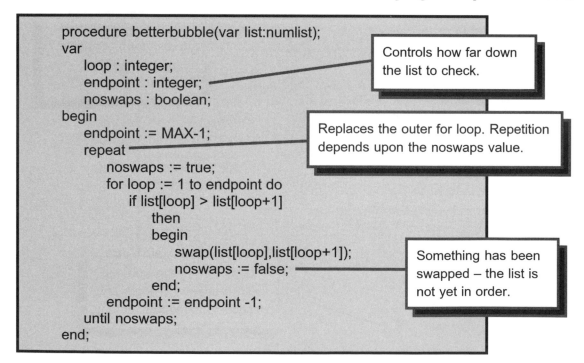

```
procedure betterbubble(var list:numlist);
var
    loop : integer;
    endpoint : integer;
    noswaps : boolean;
begin
    endpoint := MAX-1;
    repeat
        noswaps := true;
        for loop := 1 to endpoint do
            if list[loop] > list[loop+1]
                then
                begin
                    swap(list[loop],list[loop+1]);
                    noswaps := false;
                end;
        endpoint := endpoint -1;
    until noswaps;
end;
```

Controls how far down the list to check.

Replaces the outer for loop. Repetition depends upon the noswaps value.

Something has been swapped – the list is not yet in order.

The top-down sort

When you think about it, the bubble technique is not the way that you would tackle a sorting job if you were doing it by hand – and looking back to the manual methods can often pay dividends. If you were sorting a set of cards by hand, you might well do it by looking through for the one that should be at the front, moving it there, then looking for the next, and so on. This method is particularly appropriate where you must – for lack of space – keep the cards in their container, just as you normally perform a sort within the array, to save memory.

Here's another disorganised list of animals.

▶   indicates the current position in the list

⇨   indicates items compared with the current position

✖   indicates the 'lowest' to be swapped with the current position

▶ cat	ant	ant	ant	
⇨ ant ✖	▶ cat	bee	bee	
⇨ dog	⇨ dog	▶ dog	cat	
⇨ bee	⇨ bee ✖	⇨ cat ✖	dog	6 tests, 3 swaps

Compare the totals here with the basic bubble sort. The differences are not great as the numbers are so small. However, with 100 items, a basic bubble would perform almost 10,000 comparison tests and up to 5,000 swaps (the better bubble would halve the comparisons); the top down sort would perform 5,000 comparisons and no more than 100 swaps. in a top down, every swap puts one item into its final place.

When you are sorting the records, keeping the number of swaps to a minimum is vital. The comparisons only use one field, but swaps move a whole record – possibly hundreds of bytes of data. If you were sorting a random access database, on the disk rather than in memory, then it is even more important to swap as little as possible.

The top down sort

```
procedure topsort(var list: numlist);

var
 lowest : arraytype;
 lowplace : integer;
 outloop : integer;
 inloop : integer;

begin
    for outloop := 1 to MAX-1 do
    begin
        lowest := list[outloop];
        lowplace := 0;
        for inloop := outloop + 1 to MAX do
        begin
            if list[inloop] < lowest
                then
                begin
                    lowest := list[inloop];
                    lowplace := inloop;
                end;
        end;
        if lowplace <> 0
            then swap(list[outloop],list[lowplace]);
    end;
end;
```

Copy the bubble sort program and replace the bubble procedure with this one – and change the call to match!

Use the value at the top of the list as an initial value for the lowest

Note the value and the position of any item lower than the current lowest – this may be changed several times during one trip down the list.

Swap the current item with the lowest.

122

Sorting records

Any of the three sort routines given in the last few pages can be readily adapted to sort the CD database (see page 100). Here are the alterations that the top down sort would need.

Start by setting up a new **type**.

```
cdbox = array[1..50] of CD;
```

You will need this to be able to pass the array as a parameter to the sort routine. Use this type when declaring the array...

```
collection: cdbox;
```

... and in the parameter of the procedure:

```
procedure topsort(var list: cdbox);
```

Within the procedure code, the main changes arise from the fact that you are now sorting on one field in a record, rather than the whole array item. Change the type of the *lowest* variable, so that it matches the field used for sorting:

```
lowest : string[40];
```

Include the field in each line that compares with or copies values to *lowest*:

```
lowest := list[outloop].artist;
...
if list[inloop].artist < lowest
...
    lowest := list[inloop].artist;
```

The loops need adjusting. Instead of MAX, the limits are determined by *counter*.

```
for outloop := 1 to counter - 2 do
    ...
    for inloop := outloop + 1 to counter - 1 do
```

The *swap* procedure is called exactly as before...

```
then  swap(list[outloop],list[lowplace]);
```

...passing two whole records for swapping. The procedure itself is unchanged, though its parameters must be changed to the CD type:

```
procedure swap (var a,b: CD);
```

Random access files

The only significant different between sequential and random access files is how you access the records on the disk. With a sequential file, you always start reading at the top of the file, and can only reach later ones by reading through to them. With a random access file, you can go directly to any record. The ability to access any given record has a major implication for how you manage your data – *there is no longer any need for an array.*

Seek and ye shall find

This is managed by the **seek** procedure. It is used in the form:

```
seek(diskfile, record_number);
```

This moves the file pointer to the given record. After a **seek**, you use a normal **read** or **write** to transfer data from or to that place in the file.

When writing records to a random access file, the simplest approach is to start at the beginning, and put them in sequence – as with a sequential file. If you build a position number into the record structure, and include this in your display, it can later be used to select records. That is the method used in the next program. It is not particularly satisfactory as you need a written index – to look up a record number – before you can access the record on disk.

A better solution is to have a separate index file which hold a key field – e.g. the person's name – and the record's position. This is may be loaded into an array for faster look-ups. Another alternative is to use mathematical techniques to derive the position number from the key field. Both involve advanced programming techniques that are beyond the scope of this book.

Take note

read and write both move the file pointer on to the next record. If you seek and read in a record for editing, you must seek again before writing it back to the disk.

Random access CDs

The following program is based on the earlier records and CDs program, but adapted to use random access and with some extra facilities added. The simplest way to create it is to take a copy of that earlier program and edit it as follows.

There is no collection array. Delete the **load** and **save** procedures, and the calls to them from the main program. There is no array to transfer data to and from.

```
for loop := 1 to counter-1 do
begin
    seek(diskfile,loop);
    read(diskfile,single);
    showone(single);
end;
```

Edit the definition of the CD type to include a variable to hold the record's position in the file. This should be of the **longint** type, as **seek** uses **longint**s (disk addresses are 4-byte numbers.)

```
type
    cd = record
        artist:string[40];
        title :string[40];
        style :char;
        rating : integer;
        filepos : longint;
    end;
```

Add this line into the **newcd** procedure. As we are adding new records in the order that they are entered, the *counter* will be the same as their position on disk.

```
        filepos := counter;
```

Similarly, add this line to **showone**, so that the user can see the record's number – this is needed for editing and deleting.

You need a new procedure to close the file at the end of the program, and some new code at the start. The very first record (at position 0) is used to store the number of records in the file. This is held in the filepos field. The current counter value must be copied there and the record written to disk before closing the file:

```
procedure closefile;
begin
    single.filepos := counter;
    seek(diskfile,0);
    write(diskfile,single);
    close(diskfile);
end;
```

The counter value is retrieved from this record at the start of the program. Note that a seek is not necessary. After a reset, the file pointer is already pointing at the first record.

```
assign(diskfile,'randcd.dat');
reset(diskfile);
read(diskfile,single);
counter := single.filepos;
```

As with the sequential file, you need boot-up lines when the program is used for the first time. Instead of the last three lines above, use:

```
rewrite(diskfile);
counter := 1;
```

The delete procedure needs a couple of adjustments. Change the *target* variable type to longint, for the **seek**.

```
target : longint;
```

Checking that the target number is valid is crucial. You could get very strange results if you tried to read non-existent records.

```
if (target >0) and (target < counter)
```

After marking a record as deleted, it must be written back to file:

```
then begin
        single.artist[1] := chr(255);
        seek(diskfile,target);
        write(diskfile,single);
    end;
```

I have included an *edit* procedure, that was not present in the sequential version of this program. Miss it out at first, adding it in only when the rest is working properly.

Records are selected for editing using a target number, as in the delete procedure. They are then read in and displayed:

```
seek(diskfile,target);
read(diskfile,single);
showone(single);
```

It would be an interesting challenge to write a routine that would allow you to edit the fields properly – i.e. to change individual characters. I've opted for a much simpler solution. The user's responses are collected in temporary variables, *tstring* and *tchar*:

```
write('Enter new name or [Enter]');
readln(tstring);
if length(tstring) > 0 then single.artist := tstring;
```

If the user presses [Enter] *tstring* will have zero length, and no change is made. If you are not using Turbo, you will have to incorporate the *length* procedure (page 90), to make this work.

With *tchar* , we can spot the [Enter] keypress by character 13:

```
if tchar <> chr(13) then single.style := tchar;
```

An [Enter] keypress will cause a crash on integer entry. We could use the *safe number entry* routine (page 98), but it is simpler to take the *rating* value in as a char. If there is a new value, it can be quickly converted into its single digit value.

```
if tchar <> chr(13)  then single.rating := ord(tchar)-48;
```

Finally, note that you must **seek** again before writing the record back to disk.

```
seek(diskfile,target);
write(diskfile,single);
```

Random access CDs

```
program randacc;

uses WinCrt;

type
    cd = record
        artist:string[40];
        title :string[40];
        style :char;
        rating : integer;
        filepos : longint;
    end;

var
    diskfile : file of CD;
    single : CD;
    counter : integer;
    choice  : char;

procedure newcd;
begin
    with single do
    begin
        write('Enter artist: ');
        readln(artist);
        write('Enter title: ');
        readln(title);
        write('Enter style (C)lassical, (J)azz, (R)ock, (F)olk: ');
        readln(style);
        write('Enter rating (0 - 9)');
        readln(rating);
        filepos := counter;
    end;

    seek(diskfile,filepos);
    write(diskfile,single);
    counter := counter + 1;
end;
```

> Specific to Turbo Pascal for Windows – change to suit your system.

> Replace if necessary with **packed array [1..40] of char**

> The position on disk should be the same as **counter**.

> Write the record to disk.

128

```
procedure showone(disk : CD);
begin
    if single.artist[1] <> chr(255)
        then  with disk do
            begin
                writeln('Record number: ',filepos);
                writeln(artist);
                writeln(title);
                writeln(style);
                writeln(rating);
            end;
end;

procedure display;
var
    loop :  integer;
begin
    for loop := 1 to counter-1 do
    begin
        seek(diskfile,loop);
        read(diskfile,single);
        showone(single);
    end;
end;

procedure search;
var
    loop : integer;
    target: string[40];
begin
    writeln('Enter artist to search for: ');
    readln(target);
    for loop := 1 to counter-1 do
    begin
        seek(diskfile,loop);
        read(diskfile,single);
        if single.artist = target
            then showone(single);
    end;
end;
```

This positions the file pointer before each read. As the records are in sequence, you could do:

```
seek(diskfile,1);
for loop := 1 to counter-1 do
    begin
        read(diskfile,single);
        showone(single);
    end;
```

129

```
procedure editrec;
var
    target : longint;
    tstring : string[40];
    tchar  : char;
begin
    write('Record number? ');
    readln(target);
    if (target >0) and (target < counter)
        then begin
                seek(diskfile,target);
                read(diskfile,single);
                showone(single);
                write('Enter new name or [Enter]');
                readln(tstring);
                if length(tstring) > 0 then single.artist := tstring;
                write('Enter new title or [Enter]');
                readln(tstring);
                if length(tstring) > 0 then single.title := tstring;
                write('Enter new style or [Enter]');
                readln(tchar);
                if tchar <> chr(13) then single.style := tchar;
                write('Enter new rating or [Enter]');
                readln(tchar);
                if tchar <> chr(13)
                    then single.rating := ord(tchar)-48;
                seek(diskfile,target);
                write(diskfile,single);
            end;
    end;

procedure deleterec;
var
    target : longint;
begin
    write('Record number? ');
    readln(target);
    if (target >0) and (target < counter)
        then begin
                single.artist[1] := chr(255);
```

Fields updated only if new values are entered.

Convert **tchar** to 0 – 9 **rating** value.

```
                seek(diskfile,target);
                write(diskfile,single);
                end;
    end;
    procedure closefile;
    begin
        single.filepos := counter;
        seek(diskfile,0);
        write(diskfile,single);
        close(diskfile);
    end;

    begin
        assign(diskfile,'randcd.dat');
        {rewrite(diskfile);}
        { counter := 1;}
        reset(diskfile);
        read(diskfile,single);
        counter := single.filepos;
        writeln('CD collection organiser');
        repeat
            writeln('New CD.................1');
            writeln('Display collection....2');
            writeln('Select by artist.......3');
            writeln('Edit an entry...........4');
            writeln('Delete an entry.......5');
            writeln('Exit.......................6');
            readln(choice);

            case choice of
                '1' :     newcd;
                '2' :     display;
                '3' :     search;
                '4' :     editrec;
                '5' :     deleterec;
                '6' :     closefile;
            end;
        until choice = '6';
    end.
```

Needed on first run, before file exists.

Store number of records in record 0

Don't forget to include the **edit** procedure in the menu.

Exercise

1. A small construction company employes a number of workers. They are paid at an hourly rate of £4 (unskilled) or £7 (skilled), with overtime (at time and a half) above 40 hours. All are self-employed contractors, which means that the firm deducts a standard 25% of all their earnings, to cover tax and national insurance.

    Design and write a program to handle the payroll. For each worker it should record the name, hourly rate, current week's pay, current week's deductions, total earnings (Year To Date) and total deductions (YTD). There should be procedures to add and delete workers, and to change their hourly rate. This data should be held in a random access file.

    For the weekly payrun, the pay clerk should enter the hours worked by each worker, and the program should display and print wage slips showing the hours worked, gross pay, deductions, net pay plus the total pay and tax to date.

Tip

Start from a copy of the CD database. It will give you the basic structure and some of the key routines.

7 Lists and pointers

Linked lists

We looked earlier (page 118) at the problems – and the work – involved in sorting lists into order. If you could *create* lists in order, *and keep them that way*, it would eliminate the delays caused by sorting. With linked lists, you have permanently sorted data. Data goes into the list in order, and the order is re-established as items are inserted and deleted later.

Put simply, a linked list consists of a set of records, each of which contains a link to the next record – and 'next' means in alphabetical or numerical order of a key field, not the order in which they were entered or stored. Here's our set of animals, organised as a linked list. They appear in the array in the order in which they were stored.

Position	Name	... other fields ...	Next
0			2
1	cat		3
2	ant		4
3	dog		-1
4	bee		1
5	*free*		6
6	...		7
7	...		8

free = 5

The *Next* field gives the *Position* of the next record. Start from 0 and follow the links until you reach –1, which indicates the end of the list. You should read 2 → 'ant' → 4 → 'bee' → 1 → 'cat' → 3 → 'dog'.

From 5 onwards, the array is empty, apart from the links connecting each to the next. In the jargon, 5 is the start of *free space*. We will use a variable called *free* to store this value.

Building a linked list

Adding an item to a linked list is simple in concept, but a bit fiddly in practice. In outline, this is the process:

> store the record in the first available free slot
>
> work through the linked list to find the place where it should fit
>
> shuffle the links so that the new item fits between existing ones

Before we turn this into code, let's have a look at how that works in our example. We will add 'bull'.

	Position	Name	... other fields ...	Next	New link
	0			2	
link ▶	1	cat		3	
	2	ant		4	
	3	dog		-1	
current ▶	4	bee		~~4~~	5
free ▶	5	**bull**		~~0~~	1
	6	*free*		7	
	7	...		8	

old free = 5   new free = 6

The 'bull' record has gone into the first free space.

```
write('Enter key field; ');
readln(list[free].key);
```

Data for the other fields would be read in at this point.

Follow the (new) links now, and you will see that the list is still in order. To do this, we moved the link 'bee' has to 'bull', and the old *free* space value to 'bee'. We'll use *current* to identify the last place before the new record, and *link* to identify the place that it points to.

To insert the new link, we have to:

> move free to current's Next, so 4 (bee) links to 5 (bull)
>
> move current's Next to free's Next, so 5 (bull) links to 1 (cat)
>
> move free's Next to free, so the new free space is 6.

Now to turn this into code.

First we have find where to insert the link. We follow the links through the list, keeping track of the current position and checking the key field at the next link, until the next is higher than the new item.

```
link := 0;      {always start at the top}
repeat
    current := link;
    link := list[current].next;
until list[link].key > list[free].key;
```

When the *link* key is 'cat' (higher than 'bull'), the *current* key is 'bee'. We can shuffle the links to bring the new item into the list.

```
nextfree := list[free].next;
list[free].next := list[current].next;
list[current].next := free;
free := nextfree;
```

Notice that you cannot use the direct assignment:

```
free := list[free].next;
```

You must retain the old value of *free* while the current next link is shuffled, and in doing that, the *list[free].next* value is overwritten. Using *nextfree* for temporary storage solves the problem.

If you look at the program on page 138, you will find that the routine is rather more complicated than shown above. To make it work, you have to add a couple of tweaks to deal with two special situations – starting a list from scratch, and inserting at the end of the list.

The starting code is straighforward. The boxed notes on the program should be enough explanation for this.

Adding at the end is trickier. The point to remember is that test is on the key field at the next linked item, but that normal inserts go after the current record. At the end of the list, the insert goes after the next linked record. These lines make the necessary adjustment.

```
if  list[link].next = -1
    then current := link;
```

Deleting from the list

Deleting a record from a linked list is simpler than inserting one. Let's start with our diagram. The situation now is that the dog has eaten the cat, so this should be removed from the list.

	Position	Name	... other fields ...			Next	New link
link ▶	0					2	
	1	**cat**				~~3~~	6
	2	ant				4	
	3	dog				-1	
	4	bee				5	
current ▶	5	bull				~~1~~	3
free ▶	6	*free*				7	
	7	...				8	

old free = 6   new free = 1

As before, we use two variables, *current* and *link*, and scan through the list comparing the link key with the target. When the target is located, *link* points to the target record, and *current* points to the one preceding it.

```
current := 0;
repeat
    link := list[current].next;
    if list[link].key < target then current := link;
until list[link].key = target ;
```

To remove the target from the list, we simply:

move link's Next to current's Next, so 5 (bull) links to 3 (dog)

The slot occupied by the 'cat' record can be returned to free space. To do this we must:

move free to link's Next, so 1 (ex-cat) links to 6 (start of free space)

move link to free, so the free space now starts at 1.

```
list[current].next := list[link].next;
list[link].next := free;
free := link;
```

Linked list

```
program linklist;

type
    datatype = char;
    keytype = integer;
    listtype = record
                    key : keytype;   {key can be string, e.g. name}
                    data : datatype; {any types / any number of fields}
                    next : integer;
              end;
var
    list : array[0..50] of listtype;
    current : integer;        {start of list}
    free : integer;          {start of free space}
    link: integer;
    choice : char;
    started : boolean;

procedure initialise;
var
    loop : integer;
begin
    for loop := 0 to 49 do
        list[loop].next := loop+1;
    free := 1;
    started := false;
end;

procedure additem;
var
    nextfree : integer;
begin
    write('Enter key field; ');
    readln(list[free].key);

    if not started
        then begin
                free := 2;
                list[1].next := -1;
                started := true;
            end
```

Link all free space.

Start free space at 1.

Set the flag to show that the list has not been started.

Other data input here.

The list is started by putting the first item in slot 1, and marking its next as the end.

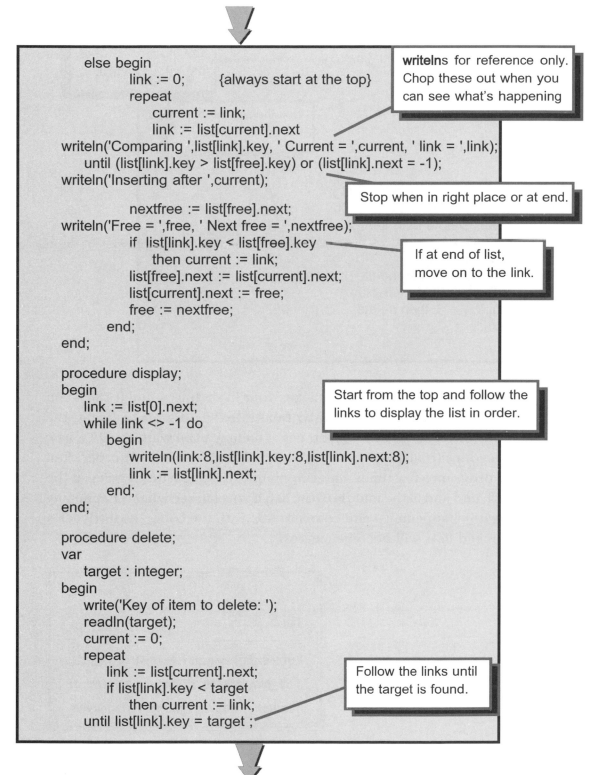

```
        else begin
            link := 0;          {always start at the top}
            repeat
                current := link;
                link := list[current].next
writeln('Comparing ',list[link].key, ' Current = ',current, ' link = ',link);
            until (list[link].key > list[free].key) or (list[link].next = -1);
writeln('Inserting after ',current);

            nextfree := list[free].next;
writeln('Free = ',free, ' Next free = ',nextfree);
            if list[link].key < list[free].key
                then current := link;
            list[free].next := list[current].next;
            list[current].next := free;
            free := nextfree;
        end;
end;

procedure display;
begin
    link := list[0].next;
    while link <> -1 do
        begin
            writeln(link:8,list[link].key:8,list[link].next:8);
            link := list[link].next;
        end;
end;

procedure delete;
var
    target : integer;
begin
    write('Key of item to delete: ');
    readln(target);
    current := 0;
    repeat
        link := list[current].next;
        if list[link].key < target
            then current := link;
    until list[link].key = target ;
```

writelns for reference only.
Chop these out when you
can see what's happening

Stop when in right place or at end.

If at end of list,
move on to the link.

Start from the top and follow the
links to display the list in order.

Follow the links until
the target is found.

```
        list[current].next := list[link].next;
        list[link].next := free;
        free := link;
    end;

    begin
        initialise;
        repeat
            writeln('Add data item.......1');
            writeln('Display  data........2');
            writeln('Delete data item....3');
            writeln('Exit...............4');
            readln(choice);
            if choice = '1' then additem;
            if choice = '2' then display;
            if choice = '3' then delete;
        until choice = '4';
    end.
```

> Cut the record out of the link sequence.

> Link the slot into the start of free space.

If thinking about linked lists makes your brain hurt – and it can – you may find it helpful to put extra **writeln**s into the program to display the states of variables at crucial times. You may even want to add a new procedure to display the array in its normal (not linked) order. Run the program a few times, entering simple data, with items going at the start, end and in the middle of the list. If you can see what is happening – as it is happening – and compare this with the code, the intricacies of linked lists will become clearer.

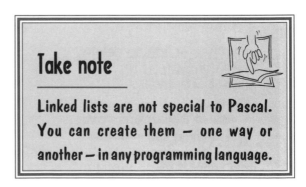

Take note

Linked lists are not special to Pascal. You can create them — one way or another — in any programming language.

Pointers

A pointer is a special type of variable. An ordinary variable is a named part of memory in which data can be stored. A pointer holds only an address, though once the pointer is brought into play it will be the address of a place where data is stored.

Pointers are created using the carat (^) symbol, specifying the type of data to which they will point. e.g.

```
var
    ptrint :  ^integer;
```

ptrint is a pointer to an integer variable.

The data that they point to is accessed using the carat again:

```
writeln(ptrint^);
```

This will display whatever value is held at the addressed place.

Assigning data to a pointer can be tricky. For a start, there may not actually be any memory in which to place it! When an ordinary variable is created, memory is assigned to it. With a pointer, the only assigned memory is a few bytes to hold an address.

You cannot assign char or any number values to pointers directly. But if the value is assigned first to a variable, you can pass the address of the variable to the pointer. The @ operator is used to get the address:

```
int := 42;
ptrint := @int;
```

After these lines, the expression *ptrint^* delivers the value held at the address pointed to by *ptrint*.

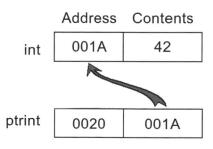

Data in string variables is also passed to pointers by assigning the address of the variable. With literal strings – and with records, as you will see shortly – you can assign directly. e.g.

　　　ptrstring^ := 'A literal string in quotes';

Notice the carat^ after the name! This assignment works because the system has allocated temporary memory storage to the string.

The program below shows the use of pointers in their simplest form.

```
program pointers;

type
    string30 = packed array[1..30] of char;
var
    int : integer;
    ptrint : ^integer;
    str  : string30;
    ptrstring : ^string30;


begin
    int := 42;
    ptrint := @int;
    writeln('Data addressed by ptrint = ',ptrint^);
    str := 'Pascal pointers made simple';
    ptrstring := @str;
    writeln('Data addressed by ptrstring = ',ptrstring^);
    ptrstring^ := 'though not that simple';
    writeln('Data assigned to ptrstring = ',ptrstring^);
end.
```

You might think, as you look at this, that there really is not much point in using pointers in these situations. You would be absolutely right. If a simple variable will do the job, use it. Pointers come into their own when you start to get into dynamic memory allocation. Read on...

Dynamic memory allocation

When you create simple variables and arrays, a fixed amount of memory is allocated to them at the start of execution. This cannot be changed during the program's run. With dynamic memory allocation, storage space is allocated from an area of spare memory called the *heap*, during the run. Though it requires more management, this approach makes for a more flexible and efficient use of memory.

Pointers are crucial to dynamic memory allocation. They are used to hold the addresses of the allocated space.

There are many memory management procedures. The key ones are:

new(var ptr: pointer)   allocates enough memory to hold the object pointed to by ptr.

dispose(var ptr:pointer)   returns allocated memory to the heap, when it is no longer required.

The following lines allocate an integer-sized space in memory, which can be accessed through *ptr^*.

```
var
    ptr : ^integer
begin
    new(ptr);
    ...
```

In practice, the object being allocated memory would not normally be a simple variable, but a record, for dynamic memory allocation is generally used to create data structures such as linked lists. In these structures, the records contain pointers to link to other records.

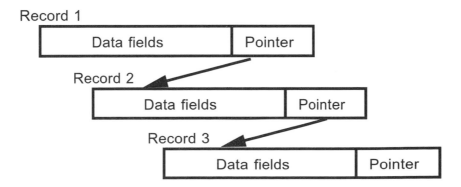

Linking with pointers

The first stage of creating a linked list with pointers, is to define the types that will be used for the variables. You need a pointer to a record, which itself contains a pointer to a record. If this sounds circular, that's because it is. Within the **type** area, you need something like this:

```
type
    ptrnode = ^node;
    node = record
            key : keytype;
            data : datatype;
            next : ptrnode;
          end;
```

Notice that *ptrnode* is defined as a pointer to *node*, which is not actually defined at that stage. This rather breaks the standard Pascal rule that you can only use terms that have already been defined, but it works. Within the *node* record, you will see the *next* field, which is defined as a pointer to records of type *node*.

The pointer field must be set up in this way, using a predefined type. You cannot define it directly. This will not work:

```
node = record
        key : keytype;
        data : datatype;
        next : ^node;
      end;
```

You will get an error on the *next : ^node;* line.

The next program demonstrates the use of pointers and dynamic memory allocation, to create a sorted linked list. The differences between this and the array-based linked list are as important as the similarities. However, the two are close enough for you to use a copy of the existing array-based program as a basis for this one.

Notice first that with dynamic memory allocation we no longer have to worry about free space – we can leave the system to manage this for us. That simplifies the insertion and deletion routines. Another thing to note is in the display procedure. You cannot write pointers to the screen, so we cannot visibly follow the route through the links.

Building the list

Where a list is in an array, it is up to you to manage the storage of data. When it being built dynamically in memory, as long as you know where it starts and where it ends, you can more or less leave the system to organise the storage and the links.

The start of the list is held in a global variable – of the *node* type defined earlier – called *top*. Memory is allocated to this in the *initalise* procedure. *top* is a dummy record. No data is stored there, except in its *next* field. This is initially set to **nil** to mark the end of the list. (**nil** or **NIL** is a Pascal constant, used to show that the pointer is pointing to nothing.)

```
new(top);
top^.next := nil;
```

New records are added to the list through the procedure newnode.

```
procedure newnode(var nextrec: ptrnode; temp : ptrnode);
begin
    new(nextrec);
    nextrec := temp;
    nextrec^.next := nil;
end;
```

This has passed to it the *next* pointer from the *current* record and the *temp* record into which data has been entered, i.e. you tell it where the record is to go, and what is to be stored there.

```
newnode(current^.next,temp);
```

Notice that the *nextrec* pointer is a **var** – this is a two-way process. The procedure will pass the address of the new record back into the *current^.next* pointer. You should also notice that the new record's *next* pointer is initially set to **nil**. This is later overwritten if the record is not placed at the end of the list. As with the arrayed linked list, the end needs special treatment. (It is even more crucial with dynamic memory allocation as mistakes cause the program to crash!)

I've deliberately skated over where the current record is – and I'm going to carry on skating for a bit longer. Let's look first at the *display* procedure. This is very similar to the version in the arrayed list program.

We start at the *top* – the one global variable in the list – and track through following the links held in the *next* fields. The loop stops when it hits the **nil** marking the end of the list.

```
link := top;
while link <> nil do
    begin
        writeln(link^.key);
        link := link^.next;
    end;
```

The *link* variable used in this is a pointer to a *node* record. *link^* is the data held at that node. *link^next* is the pointer to the following node.

Tip

It is important to remember that in a dynamically allocated structure the only record that you can reach directly is the one at the top. The rest can only be reached through the sequence of pointers from one to the next. This is totally different from an array, where – as long as you know the subscript – you can access any element directly.

You find the same tracking in the additem procedure. Here both *current* and *link* are pointers to *node* records, as is *temp*, into which data is entered.

```
link := top;
while (link <> nil) and (link^.key < temp^.key) do
    begin
        current := link;
        link := link^.next;
    end;
```

current is always one step behind *link* as it tracks through the list. So, when *link* overshoots the place where *temp* should be inserted, and stops the loop, *current* is the node to which the new node should be linked. Linking involves the same kind of shuffling that you saw in the arrayed version.

```
ptrlink:= current^.next;
newnode(current^.next,temp);
link := current^.next;
link^.next := ptrlink;
```

Suppose we had a list containing the adjacent records 'cat' and 'fox'. Watch what happens when we insert 'dog' between them.

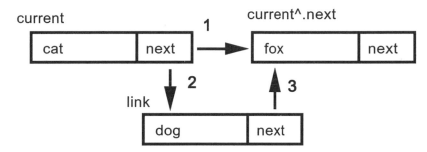

1   Initially 'cat' (*current*) points to 'fox' (*current^.next*). This address is copied into *ptrlink*.

2   *newnode* creates a new record for 'dog' and passes its address back to *current^.next* overwriting the 'fox' address. The new address is copied into *link*, so that *link* now points to 'dog'.

3   The address held in *ptrlink* is then copied to the pointer at *link^.next*.

Deleting links

This is easier than insertion. It is also easier than deletion from an arrayed list, as we don't have to worry about organising free space.

Having located the target record, so that its address is in link, all we have to do is copy the link^.next pointer back to current^.next.

```
current^.next := link^.next;
```

That takes the record out of the list. To return the record's space to the free memory of the heap, we use dispose.

```
dispose(link);
```

That's it! Now let's see how it all fits together. Don't type it in from scratch. Use a copy of the arrayed version as a base.

Linked by pointers

```
program linkpoint;

type
    datatype = char;
    keytype = integer;
    ptrnode = ^node;
    node = record
            key : keytype;
            data : datatype;
            next : ptrnode;
        end;
var
    top : ptrnode;
    current : ptrnode;
    choice : char;

procedure initialise;
begin
    new(top);
    top^ .next := nil;
end;

procedure newnode(var nextrec: ptrnode; temp : ptrnode);
begin
    new(nextrec);
    nextrec := temp;
    nextrec^.next := nil;
end;

procedure additem;
var
    temp : ptrnode;
    link: ptrnode;
    ptrlink: pointer;
    nextfree : integer;

begin
    new(temp);
    write('Enter key field: ');
    readln(temp^.key);
```

> Remember that the key field can be any type, and you can have any number of fields.

> Will point to the start of the list.

> Memory allocated and the address passed to **nextrec**.

> Data for other fields entered at this point.

148

```
        link := top;
        while (link <> nil) and (link^.key < temp^.key) do
            begin
                current := link;
                link := link^.next;
            end;
        if link = nil
            then newnode(current^.next,temp)
        else begin
            ptrlink:= current^.next;
            newnode(current^.next,temp);
            link := current^.next;
            link^.next := ptrlink;
        end;
    end;

procedure display;
var
    link : ptrnode;
begin
    link := top;
    while link^.next <> nil do
        begin
            link := link^.next;
            writeln(link^.key);
        end;
end;

procedure delete;
var
    target : keytype;
    link : ptrnode;
begin
    write('Key of item to delete: ');
    readln(target);
    current := top;
    repeat
        link := current^.next;
        if link^.key < target
            then current := link;
    until (link^.key = target) or (link = nil);
```

Start at the top.

Inserting at end, no need to adjust pointers.

Shuffle pointers to fit the new record into the list.

Remember these are both pointers to node records.

Stop when found or at end or list.

```
        current^.next := link^.next;
        dispose(link);
end;

procedure save;
var
    link : ptrnode;
    temp : node;
begin
    assign(diskfile,'linklist.dta');
    rewrite(diskfile);
    link := top;
    while link^.next <> nil do
        begin
            link := link^.next;
            write(diskfile,link^);
        end;
      close(diskfile)
end;

procedure load;
var
    temp: ptrnode;
    link : ptrnode;
    ptrlink : ptrnode;
begin
    assign(diskfile,'linklist.dta');
    reset(diskfile);
    while not eof(diskfile) do
        begin
            new(temp);
            read(diskfile,temp^);
            link := top;
            while (link <> nil) and (link^.key < temp^.key) do
                begin
                    current := link;
                    link := link^.next;
                end;
            ptrlink := current^.next;
            newnode(current^.next,temp);
            link := current^.next;
```

This is based on the **display** routine, but note that you **write** (not **writeln**) the whole record, identified as the data at the pointer – **link^**

This uses the same techniques as in **additem**, but **read**s whole records from disk into the pointer's allocated memory at **temp^**

150

```
                link^.next := ptrlink;
            end;
    end;

    begin
        initialise;
        load;
        repeat
            writeln('Add data item.......1');
            writeln('Display data..........2');
            writeln('Delete data item....3');
            writeln('Exit.......................4');
            readln(choice);
            if choice = '1' then additem;
            if choice = '2' then display;
            if choice = '3' then delete;
        until choice = '4';
        save;
    end.
```

When you first run the program, put brackets around {load;} as there will be no file to open.

Exercise

1   How much memory is available on your system for dynamic memory allocation? It may be more than you think.

Write a program to test the limits. It should use the **new** procedure repeatedly, displaying a count of the repetitions. Defining a record size of around 1kb will give you a fairly accurate measure of memory.

Take note

This kind of memory-grabbing program is potentially dangerous! If you are working on a desktop PC, save the program — and any other data files that may be open in other applications — before you run it. If you are working on a multi-user system or network, check with your system administrator before trying it!

8 Introducing Turbo Pascal

The environment

Turbo Pascal's IDE (Integrated Development Environment) enables you to edit, compile, debug and run your programs from within one window. Any number of program files can be open at once, so that you can easily copy blocks of code from one to another. This also simplifies cross-checking where you are developing a set of programs as an integrated package.

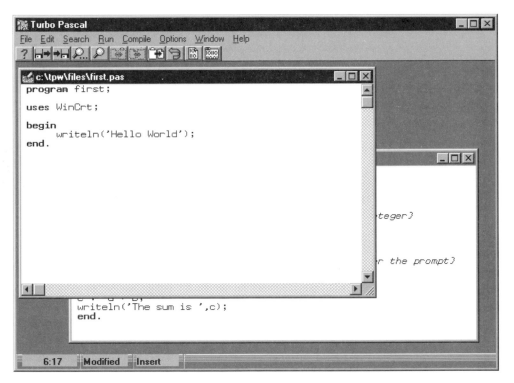

The Speedbar

All the IDE's facilities can be reached through the menu system, and the more comonly used ones are present as buttons on the Speedbar.

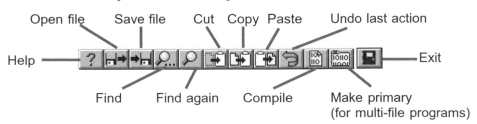

The menu system

The File menu

You will find here the Windows-standard range of options for opening, saving and printing files. Recently-used files can be selected by a single click on their names.

Check that **Printer Setup** runs correctly on your system before attempting to use it during a work session – it hangs Turbo Pascal on my Windows 95 machine.

The Edit menu

This offers the normal Cut, Copy and Paste (and lets you Clear the clipboard), and also holds an excellent **Undo** command. This stores all your recent moves and edits, allowing you to track back and remove 'corrections' that turned out to be mistakes!

Note that Turbo has its own Cut and Paste shortcuts, using [Ctrl] [Shift] [Del] and [Ins] rather than the [Ctrl] + [X]/[C]/[V] combinations used by most Windows applications.

The Search menu

Use the options here to simplify editing and debugging. **Replace** is particularly useful for doing global changes on variable names, and **Find** will let you track variables through the code, so that you can make sure that you are still spelling the name the same way on line 500 as on line1.

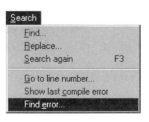

The **Find error** routine pinpoints the location of run-time errors. This is covered in *Debugging* on page 158.

155

Run

The **Run** option compiles (if necessary) and runs the current program. **Debugger** starts up the Turbo Debugger (mainly of interest to advanced programmers using in-line assembler or accessing system variables). Use **Parameters** to start up a program with command line parameters.

Compile

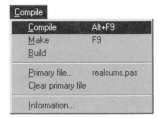

The main option here is **Compile**. Use this to check your code for syntax errors.

Make, **Build** and the **Primary** files options are used where a program is created out of several separate program and unit files.

Information will tell you the size of your current compiled program and how much memory is used for variable storage.

Options

Use this to tell Turbo which **Directories** to use for storage, and to control the screen display (See page 157 for more on these.) The **Compiler** and **Linker** options are for advanced users.

Note that you can save – and open – Option files, if you want different Directory settings for the different applications you are developing.

Help

Help is readily available. Amongst other things, you will find the technical specifications for all of Turbo's functions and procedures here, as well as some sample programs to show how they are used.

Setting directories

The directory for your code (.PAS) files can be set when you save them, or you can set the default directory in the Properties dialog box. (Open this from the Turbo shortcut in the Start menu of Windows 95, or the icon in Program Manager in Windows 3.1.)

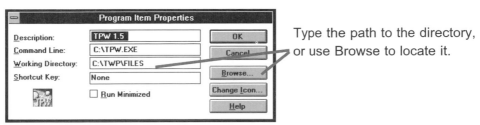

Type the path to the directory, or use Browse to locate it.

When programs are compiled into .EXE or TPU (unit) files, they are stored in the directory set in the **Directories** dialog box. Use the **Options** menu to open this and type in the path to your chosen directory. When you get deeper into Turbo Pascal and start to create programs that call on unit, resource or other files, you will need to come back to this box to set the paths to the directories in which you are keeping these.

Set this path early on, and the rest when you need to.

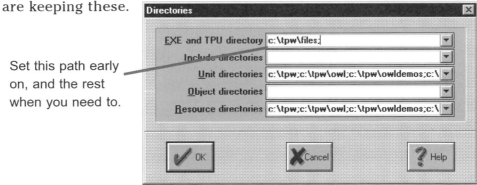

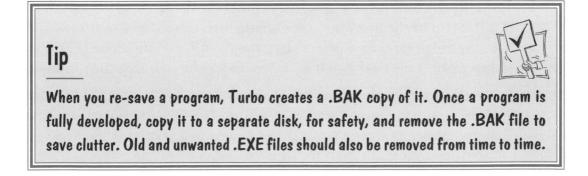

Tip

When you re-save a program, Turbo creates a .BAK copy of it. Once a program is fully developed, copy it to a separate disk, for safety, and remove the .BAK file to save clutter. Old and unwanted .EXE files should also be removed from time to time.

Debugging in Turbo Pascal

Syntax errors

When attempting to compile a program, Turbo Pascal will stop at the first error that it finds. You will see the bugged line highlighted, and an error report in the status bar at the bottom of the screen.

```
Turbo Pascal - [c:\tpw\files\titles2.pas]
File  Edit  Search  Run  Compile  Options  Window  Help

begin
 {get data}
    write('Enter age in years: ');
    readln(age);
    write('Sex (M/F): ');
    readln(sex);
    write('Marital status (M)arried, (S)ingle: ');
    readln(status);
{test and store results}
    if age < 18
      then young := true
      else young := false;
    if (sex = 'M') or (sex = 'm')                    {male?}
      then male := true ;
      else male := false;
    if (status = 'M') or (status = 'm')              {married?}
      then married := true
      else married := false;
{output appropriate form of address}
    if male and young then Writeln('call him Master');
    if male and not young then Writeln('call him Mr');
    if not male and married then Writeln('call her Mrs');
    if not male and not married and young then Writeln('call her Miss');
    if not male and not married and not young then Writeln('call her Ms');
end.

25:9      Modified   Insert    Error 113: Error in statement.
```

As in other Pascals, error reports should only be taken as a guide. In this illustration, for example, the error is the presence of a semi-colon at the end of the line above the highlighted one. This has turned the **if...the...else** structure into an **if ... then**, with a floating else. **Error in statement** is the best way that the compiler can describe the problem.

The good thing about this approach is that you don't have to hunt through the program to find your errors. The flip side is that, as each compilation attempt will only throw up one bug, it can take quite a few goes to get clear through to the end.

Run-time errors

Those errors that produce strange results can only be solved by the same methods outlined earlier, but Turbo is very good for finding those that result in crashes.

1   When the program hits an error that brings it to a stop, the system will report an error number and – more importantly – the memory address it which it occurred. Make a note of the numbers! They may not mean much to you, but the system can use them to locate the error.

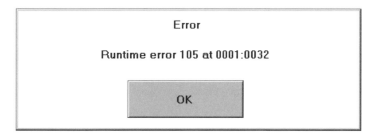

2   Open the Search menu and select Find error.

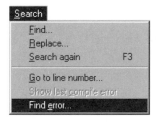

3   Type the address numbers into the dialog box – there will always be 2 sets of 4 hexadecimal digits, separated by a colon.

The system will highlight the line in the text corresponding to the address. That's where the crash is arising.

Getting Help

There are several ways into the Help system. Which one is best depends on what you are doing at the time. If you are about to tackle a new aspect of the system and need to how it works – or even to know what is available – use the Help menu and select a heading from there.

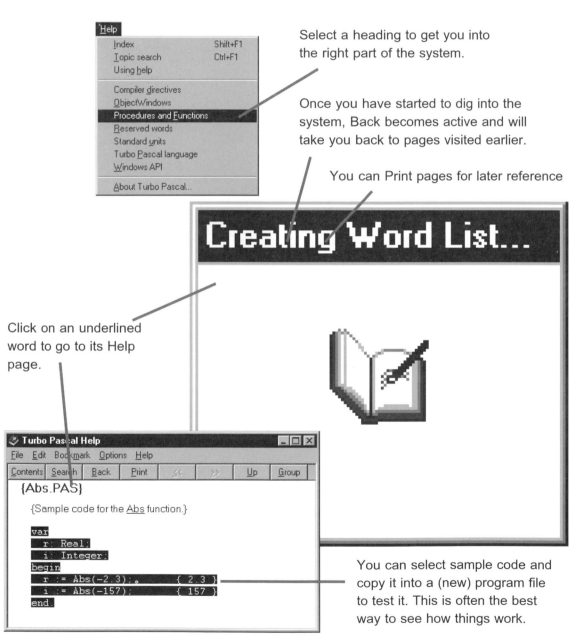

Select a heading to get you into the right part of the system.

Once you have started to dig into the system, Back becomes active and will take you back to pages visited earlier.

You can Print pages for later reference

Click on an underlined word to go to its Help page.

You can select sample code and copy it into a (new) program file to test it. This is often the best way to see how things work.

Help on key words

If you have used a procedure or function in your program and need help with it – either because it won't compile or it gives strange results – click the editing cursor into the word and press [Ctrl]-[F1].

This opens the Help page for that word directly, avoiding the trip through the menu and the contents lists.

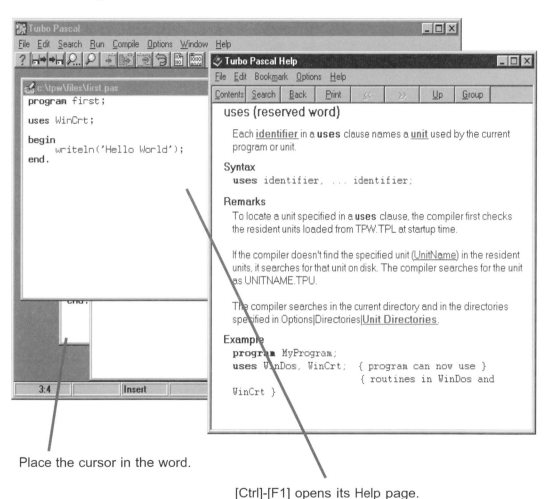

Place the cursor in the word.

[Ctrl]-[F1] opens its Help page.

9 Answers to exercises

Chapter 1

1   The simplest way to move text across the screen is to position a space at the start of the line – the alternative involves counting the characters.

```
program nameadd;
begin
    writeln('Butterworth-Heinemann');
    writeln(' ':4,'Linacre House');
    writeln(' ':8,'Jordan Hill');
    writeln(' ':12,'Oxford OX2 8DP');
end.
```

2   You could do this by a series of lines of the type:

```
c := a + b:
writeln(a:0:2,' + ',b:0:2,' = ', c:0:2);
```

Or you can simply get the writeln to calculate and display.

```
program realnums;
var
    a,b: real;
begin
    write('Enter a number: ');
    readln(a);
    write('and another: ');
    readln(b);
    writeln(a:0:2,' + ',b:0:2,' = ', a+b:0:2);
    writeln(a:0:2,' - ',b:0:2,' = ', a-b:0:2);
    writeln(a:0:2,' * ',b:0:2,' = ', a*b:0:2);
    writeln(a:0:2,' / ',b:0:2,' = ', a/b:0:2);
end.
```

3   You could calculate the paint directly from the height, width and length figures, but it is best to calculate the areas separately first. If you get odd results, you can then check the intermediate calculations.

```
program realnums;
var
    height, width, length: real;
    ceiling, walls : real;
    paint1,paint2: real;
begin
    write('Enter the height in metres: ');
    readln(height);
    write('Enter the width in metres: ');
    readln(width);
```

```
        write('Enter the length in metres: ');
        readln(length);
        ceiling := width * length;
        paint1 := ceiling /5;
        walls := (length + width) * 2 * height;
        paint2 := walls/5;
        writeln('Ceiling needs ',paint1:0:1,' litres');
        writeln('Walls need ',paint2:0:1,' litres');
    end.
```

Chapter 2

1   Each line of the display needs a **write**, with a field width, to set the start position for the stars, then a loop to write the stars, and finally a **writeln** to move on to the next. The field width decreases by 1 each time, and the sequence of stars is 1,3,5,7,9,11, which is 2 * outer − 1.

```
program starloop;
var
    outer, inner : integer;
begin
    for outer := 1 to 8 do
        begin
            write(' ':40-outer);
            for inner := 1 to 2 * outer -1 do
                write('*');
            writeln;
        end;
end.
```

2   There are several ways to tackle this. I have used a **repeat** and two **ifs**. You could use a **while** for the loop, and **if... else** for the feedback.

```
program guessing;
var
    x, guess  : integer;
begin
    randomize;
    x := random(100)+1;
    repeat
        write('Guess the number');
        readln(guess);
        if guess > x then writeln('Too high');
```

```
        if guess < x then writeln('Too low');
    until guess = x;
    writeln('Well done');
end.
```

3   A **case** statement offers the neatest way to handle the multiple
    branching here. Each set of months (31-day, 30-day and February) can
    then be checked with a single **if** statement. In February, we also have
    to look out for leap years. A **mod** division on the year number will
    show whether or not it is a leap year, and this can be used to set a flag.

```
program validate;
var
    year,month,day : integer;
    leap, valid  : boolean;
begin
    write('Enter the year number: ');
    readln(year);
    if year mod 4 = 0 then leap := true else leap := false;
    write('Enter the month number: ');
    readln(month);
    write('Enter the day number: ');
    readln(day);
    valid := false;
    case month of
        1,3,5,7,8,10,12   : if day <= 31 then valid := true;
        4,6,9,11          : if day <= 30 then valid := true;
        2                 : if leap and (day <= 29) then valid := true
                            else if day <= 28 then valid := true;
    end;
    if valid
        then writeln('Date is valid')
    else writeln('Invalid date');
end.
```

4   Digits, space and control characters can all be tested readily by
    simple if statements . Letters present a bit more of a problem, as there
    are two sets of limits to check. Notice the brackets in that line. They
    are essential! Trying to pick out symbols would be hard work, as they
    are scattered throughout the ASCII set. However, if you use one long,
    multi-nested if ... else statement, the symbols are easily found. They
    are what are left after everything else has been taken out.

```
program characters;
var
    c : char;
begin
    write('Enter a character; ');
    readln(c);
    if  c = ' '
        then writeln('Space')
    else if (c >= '0') and (c <= '9')
            then writeln('Digit')
            else if ((c >= 'A') and (c <= 'Z')) or ((c >= 'a') and (c <= 'z'))
                    then writeln('Letter')
                    else if ord(c) < 32
                            then writeln('Control character')
                            else writeln('Symbol');
end.
```

Chapter 3

1   The key trick here is to use **round()** to convert the reals to integers
     when using them as the end value for the loop.

```
program barchart1;
var
    nums : array[1..10] of real;
    loop, star  : integer;
begin
    for loop := 1 to 10 do
        begin
            write('Enter value ',loop);
            read(nums[loop]);
        end;
    for loop := 1 to 10 do
        begin
            for star := 1 to round(nums[loop]) do
                write('*');
            writeln(nums[loop]:0:2);
        end;
end.
```

2   To find the largest value, we need a variable (*biggest* in this program)
     which is initially set to 0, then revalued each time a larger value is
     found. This can be done in a separate loop, or during the input stage.

For scaling, you take the screen width and divide that by the biggest to give a scale value; e.g. 80/160 would give a *scale* of 0.5. Each number is then multiplied by this before being used as the end value for the *star* loop. This could also be done directly within the **for** line ...

```
for start := 1 to round(nums[loop] * 75 / biggest do
```

The calculations could be reversed on this, so that *scale = biggest/ width*. This would then be used to divide the number before charting.

```
program barchart2;
var
    nums : array[1..10] of real;
    loop : integer;
    star : integer;
    biggest : real;
    scale : real;
    length : integer;
begin
    biggest := 0;
    for loop := 1 to 10 do
        begin
            write('Enter value ',loop);
            read(nums[loop]);
            if nums[loop] > biggest then biggest := nums[loop];
        end;
    scale := 75/biggest;
    for loop := 1 to 10 do
        begin
            length := round(nums[loop] * scale);
            for star := 1 to length do
                write('*');
            writeln(nums[loop]:0:2);
        end;
end.
```

3   In this design, everything flows from the fact that the random numbers will serve as subscripts to an array[1..6] of integer.

```
program randtest;

var
    numbers : array [1..6] of integer;
    loop : integer;
```

```
        x    : integer;

begin
    for loop := 1 to 6 do
        numbers[loop] := 0;
    randomize;
    for loop := 1 to 600 do
        begin
            x := random(6)+1;
            numbers[x] := numbers[x] + 1;
        end;
    for loop := 1 to 6 do
        writeln('Value ',loop,' occurrences ',numbers[loop]);
end.
```

4   When a set is assigned to a constant, it is defined in exactly the same
    way as when it is written directly into the code.

```
program settest2;
const
    digits = [0..127];
    validans = ['Y','y','N','n'];
    nono = ['N','n'];
var
    n : integer;
    yesno: char;

begin
    repeat
        writeln('Enter digit');
        readln(n);
        if n in digits
            then writeln('n is between 0 and 127');
        write('Again? ');
        readln(yesno);
        while not (yesno in validans) do
        begin
            write('Enter Y or N ');
            readln(yesno);
        end;
    until yesno in nono;
end.
```

5 Using sets greatly simplifies this kind of job. Compare the clarity of the **if** tests in this program with the one in Chapter 2.

```
program characters2;
var
  c : char;
begin
    repeat
        write('Enter a character; ');
        readln(c);
        if  c = ' ' then writeln('Space')
        else if c in ['0'..'9'] then writeln('Digit')
            else if c in ['A'..'Z','a'..'z'] then writeln('Letter')
                else if ord(c) < 32
                    then writeln('Control character')
                    else writeln('Symbol');
    until c = 'x'
  end.
```

Chapter 4

1 To write this, just follow the pattern of the *factorial* function.

```
function  power(n:real;p:integer):real;
begin
    if p=1
        then power := n
        else power := n * power(n,p-1);
end;
```

2 As you will be passing the array as a parameter, define the structure as a new **type** at the start of the program – and remember to use **var** where parameters are to pass new values back.

Note that *min* and *max* are almost identical – cut and paste the code!

```
program stats;

type
    dataset = array [1..10] of real;
var
    nums : dataset;
    counter :  integer;
    choice : char;
```

```pascal
procedure getdata(var n:dataset);
begin
    counter := 0;
    repeat
        counter := counter + 1;
        write('Enter next number or 0 to stop: ');
        readln(n[counter]);
    until (n[counter] = 0) or (counter = 10);
    if nums[counter] = 0 then counter := counter -1;
end;


function total(n:dataset):real;
var
    loop : integer;
    temp : real;
begin
    temp := 0;
    for loop := 1 to counter do
        temp := temp + n[loop];
    total := temp;
end;

function average(n:dataset):real;
begin
    average := total(n) / counter;
end;

function max(n:dataset):real;
var
    loop: integer;
    biggest: real;
begin
    biggest := n[1];
    for loop := 2 to counter do
        if n[loop] > biggest then biggest := n[loop];
    max := biggest;
end;

function min(n:dataset):real;
var
    loop: integer;
    lowest: real;
```

```
begin
    lowest := n[1];
    for loop := 2 to counter do
        if n[loop] < lowest then lowest := n[loop];
    min := lowest;
end;

procedure barchart(n:dataset);
var
    loop : integer;
    star : integer;
begin
    for loop := 1 to counter do
        begin
            for star := 1 to round(n[loop]) do
                write('*');
            writeln(n[loop]:0:2);
        end;
end;

begin
    repeat
        writeln('Enter data.........1');
        writeln('Chart results......2');
        writeln('Total..................3');
        writeln('Average.............4');
        writeln('Maximum............5');
        writeln('Minimum............6');
        writeln('Exit....................7');
        readln(choice);
        case choice of
            '1' :     getdata(nums);
            '2' :     barchart(nums);
            '3' :     writeln('The total is ',total(nums):0:2);
            '4' :     writeln('The average is ',average(nums):0:2);
            '5' :     writeln('The maximum is ',max(nums):0:2);
            '6' :     writeln('The minimum is ',min(nums):0:2);
            '7' : ;
        else writeln('Invalid choice')
        end;
    until choice = '7';
end.
```

Chapter 5

1   The left string procedure is simply a matter of copying characters from the start of the old string. If you want to idiot-proof your procedure you should check that the string has at least as many characters as are being copied.

```
procedure leftstr(var newstr: string80; oldstr: string80; num:integer);
var
    loop : integer;
begin
    if num > length(oldstr)
    then writeln('Error! You cannot have that many')
    else
        begin
            for loop := 1 to num do
                newstr[loop] := oldstr[loop];
            newstr[loop] := chr(0);
        end;
end;
```

Copying from the right end of the string is trickier. You first find the length of the string, then work back to find the start point. This will be *length – number + 1*; e.g. to copy 6 from the end of 'Pascal Made Simple', (18 characters), you start at 13 (18 – 6 + 1) to get the last 6.

You might like to add your own idiot-proofing to this procedure.

```
procedure rightstr(var newstr:string80; oldstr:string80; num:integer);
var
    loop : integer;
    len : integer;
    startat: integer;
    count : integer;
begin
    len := length(oldstr);
    startat := len - num + 1;
    count := 1;
    for loop := startat to len do
        begin
            newstr[count] := oldstr[loop];
            count := count + 1;
        end;
    newstr[count] := chr(0);
end;
```

2   To convert a whole string to upper case, we just run it through a loop, sending each character in turn to the upper function.

```
function upper(c:char):char;
begin
    if c in ['a'..'z']
     then upper := chr(ord(c)-32)
     else upper := c;
end;

procedure upstring(var s:string80);
var
  loop: integer;

begin
    loop := 1;
    while s[loop] <> chr(0) do
        s[loop] := upper(s[loop]);
end;
```

3   The simplest way to tackle this is to create a *lower* function, on the same lines as *upper*. Pass the first character of the string to upper, then loop the rest through lower to get a properly capitalised name.

```
function upper(c:char):char;
begin
    if c in ['a'..'z'] then upper := chr(ord(c)-32)
    else upper := c;
end;

function lower(c:char):char;
begin
    if c in ['A'..'Z'] then lower := chr(ord(c)+32)
    else lower := c;
end;

procedure proper(var s:string80);
var
    loop: integer;
begin
    s[1] := upper(s[1]);
    for loop := to length(s) do
        s[loop] := lower(s[loop]);
end;
```

4 This version uses two **if** lines to find the value of the character. You might like to add a third to handle lower case 'a' to 'f' digits. What else would need changing to make the function handle these?

```
program hex;

{include your string procedures if necessary}

var
   temp: string80; {or string[80] in Turbo}
   n : longint;

function gethex(s : string80):integer;
var
   loop : integer;
   temp : integer;
   c    : char;
   cval : integer;
begin
   temp := 0;
   loop := 1;
   c := s[loop];
   while c in ['0'..'9','A'..'F']  do
   begin
      if c in ['0'..'9']
          then cval := ord(c) - 48;
      if c in ['A'..'F']
          then cval := ord(c) - 55;
      temp := temp * 16 + cval;
      loop := loop + 1;
      c := s[loop];
   end;
   gethex := temp;
end;

begin
   write('Enter hex number: ');
   stringin(temp);
   n := gethex(temp);
   writeln('The denary equivalent is ',n);
end.
```

Chapter 6

This is by far the longest program we have had so far. Of course, if you were producing a payroll program for commercial use, it would be far longer once you had added all the vital error-trapping routines and other refinements.

With any program of this kind of size, develop it in sections. Get the input and display routines working first, then start to add the procedures to edit, calculate and output results.

```
program randacc2;

type
    employee = record
        name :string[40];
        hourly : real;
        pay : real;
        tax : real;
        payYTD : real;
        taxYTD : real;
        filepos : longint;
    end;

var
    diskfile : file of employee;
    single : employee;
    counter : integer;
    choice  : char;

procedure newemployee;
begin
    with single do begin
        write('Enter name: ');
        readln(name);
        write('Enter hourly rate: ');
        readln(hourly);
        filepos := counter;
        seek(diskfile,filepos);
        write(diskfile,single);
    end;
    counter := counter + 1;
end;
procedure showone(disk : employee);
```

Include your stringin and stringout procedures if necessary, and adjust all the **name** lines to match.

As **tax** is 25% of **pay**, you don't need to store these. They could be calculated as needed.

```
begin
    if length(single.name) > 0 then    { don't display deleted records}
        with disk do begin
            writeln('Payroll number: ',filepos);
            writeln('Name: ',name);
            writeln('Hourly rate: ',hourly:0:2);
            writeln('Pay to date: ',payYTD:0:2);
            writeln('Deduction to date: ',taxYTD:0:2);
        end;
end;

procedure display;
var
    loop :  integer;
begin
    for loop := 1 to counter-1 do
        begin
            seek(diskfile,loop);
            read(diskfile,single);
            showone(single);
        end;
end;

procedure editrec;
var
    target : longint;
begin
    write('Worker number? ');
    readln(target);
    if (target >0) and (target < counter)
        then begin
            seek(diskfile,target);
            read(diskfile,single);
            showone(single);
            write('Enter new hourly rate');
            readln(single.hourly);
            seek(diskfile,target);
            write(diskfile,single);
        end;
end;
```

```pascal
procedure deleterec;
var
   target : longint;
   reply  : char;
begin
   write('Record number? ');
   readln(target);
   if (target >0) and (target < counter)
      then begin
              single.name := '';
              seek(diskfile,target);
              write(diskfile,single);
          end;
end;

procedure payrun;
var
   hours : real;
   loop : integer;
begin
   for loop := 1 to counter - 1 do
   begin
      seek(diskfile,loop);
      read(diskfile,single);
      with single do begin
         writeln('Hours worked by ',name);
         readln(hours);
         if hours <= 40
            then pay := hours * hourly
            else pay := 40 * hourly + (hours - 40) * hourly * 1.5;
         tax := pay * 0.25;
         payYTD := payYTD + pay;
         taxYTD := taxYTD + tax;
      end;
      seek(diskfile,loop);
      write(diskfile,single);
   end;
end;

procedure showpay;
var
   loop :  integer;
   totpay,tottax : real;
```

```
begin
    totpay := 0;
    tottax := 0;
    writeln('Payroll No.  Name        Gross   Deductions  Net');
    for loop := 1 to counter-1 do
    begin
        seek(diskfile,loop);
        read(diskfile,single);
        if length(single.name) > 0 then
            with single do begin
                writeln(filepos:12,name:12,pay:10:2,tax:10:2,pay-tax:8:2);
                totpay := totpay + pay;
                tottax := tottax + tax;
            end;
    end;
    writeln('Totals':24,totpay:8:2,tottax:8:2,totpay-tottax:8:2);
end;

procedure wageslip;
var
    loop :  integer
    output : text;
    net : real

begin
    assign(output,'printout.prn');
    rewrite(output);
    for loop := 1 to counter-1 do
    begin
        seek(diskfile,loop);
        read(diskfile,single);
        writeln(output,'Payroll No.  Name        Gross   Deductions  Net
GrossYTD   DeductionsYTD');
        net := single.pay - single.tax;
        with single do
            writeln(output,filepos:12,name:12,pay:10:2,tax:10:2,
net:10:2,payYTD:10:2,taxYTD:10:2);
        writeln(output);
        writeln(output);
    end;
    close(output);
end;
```

> In some versions of Pascal, all files must be declared globally. If your printout file does not appear, move this line to the top of the program.

> Overlong lines!

```
procedure closefile;
begin
    single.filepos := counter;
    seek(diskfile,0);
    write(diskfile,single);
    close(diskfile);
end;

begin
    assign(diskfile,'employee.dat');
    {rewrite(diskfile);    }          {needed for initial boot}
    reset(diskfile);
    read(diskfile,single);
    counter := single.filepos;
    {counter := 1;  }                 {needed for inital boot}
    writeln('Payroll');
    repeat
        writeln('New employee.............1');
        writeln('Display all..............2');
        writeln('Search for employee......3');
        writeln('Edit an hourly rate......4');
        writeln('Delete an entry..........5');
        writeln('Weekly payrun............6');
        writeln('Display pay and totals...7');
        writeln('Print wage slips.........8');
        writeln('Exit.....................9');
        readln(choice);
        case choice of
            '1' :    newemployee;
            '2' :    display;
            '3' :    search;
            '4' :    editrec;
            '5' :    deleterec;
            '6' :    payrun;
            '7' :    showpay;
            '8' :    wageslip;
            '9' :    closefile;
        end;
    until choice = '9';
end.
```

Chapter 7

Adding new nodes is much simpler here than with the list, as we are not trying to sort them into order. It is not even necessary to link the nodes, though we may as well as that carries no memory overhead.

A **repeat ... until false** loop will keep the program going until it crashes.

```
program DMAtest;

type
    ptrnode = ^node;
    node = record
        key : packed array[1..1020] of char;
        next : ptrnode;
    end;
   {pointers take 4 bytes; this array takes just over 1020 = total 1kb}

var
    top : ptrnode;
    temp : ptrnode;
    count : longint;

begin
    new(top);
    count := 0;
    repeat
        new(temp);                    {allocate memory}
        top^.next := temp;            {link to last}
        top := temp;                  {move the link on}
        count := count + 1;
        writeln(count);
    until false
end.
```

10 Language summary

Reserved words

These are used to create the structure of Pascal programs and may not be used for names of variables, procedures or functions.

and Links two arguments in a logical test. Both must be true for the test to give a true result. (Page 36)

array Used to define a compound variable – one that can store many items, all identified by the same name but different subscripts. (Chapter 3)

begin Marks the start of a block of code. (Pages 4, 25)

case ... of Branching mechanism. Used in preference to **if** where the program flow may go in one of several different directions. (Page 42)

const Marks the start of the area in which constants are defined. (Page 18)

div Operator for integer division, giving the number of times one number will go into another. (Page 16)

do Used in conjunction with **for**, **while** and **with**.(Pages 24, 32 and 113)

downto Used in a **for** loop to decrement the control variable. (Page 27)

else Optional extension to **if** and **case**, to handle those situations not covered by positive selections. (Page 38 and 42)

end Marks the end of a **begin** block, or a **case** or **record** structure. (Pages 25, 42 and 112)

file Used to define a variable that handles a link to a disk file. (Page 104)

for ... to ... do Causes the program to loop around a block of code for a given number of times. (Page 24)

function Marks the start of a function. (Page 78)

goto Jumps to a point in the program marked by a **label**. (Page 44)

if ... then Tests a condition and performs the statement(s) after **then**, if the test proves *true*. Can include an **else** to handle *false* results. (Page 34)

in Operator for comparing a value with the contents of a set. (Page 60)

label Used to create a label for a **goto** jump. (Page 44)

mod Gives the remainder from an integer division. (Page 16)

nil Assigned to a pointer that has not been given a memory address. (Page 145)

not Operator that reverses the truth of a logical expression. (Page 36)

of Part of the **case** statement. (Page 42)

or Links two arguments in a logical test. The test is true if either or both of the arguments are true. (Page 36)

packed Used to define a char array, where it will hold strings of text. (Page 56)

procedure Marks the start of a procedure. (Page 72)

program Marks the start of a program. (Page 4)

record Used in defining record structures in the **type** or **var** areas. (Page 112)

repeat Marks the start of a loop, ended by an **until** line. (Page 30)

set of Can be used to define a set of values as a new **type**.

then Part of the **if** statement. (Page 34)

to Part of the normal **for** loop, where the control variable increments each time round. (Page 24)

type Marks the start of the area for defining new variable types. (Page 63)

until The bottom line of a **repeat** loop, holding the exit test. (Page 30)

var Marks the start of the area for variable declaration. (Page 11)

while ... do Starts a loop that repeats while the test in the line is true. (Page 32)

with ... do Attaches a record identifier to any field variables in following statement(s). (Page 113)

xor Links two logical arguments. The test is true if one or other – but not both – of the arguments are true.

Turbo Pascal reserved words

These are not part of the standard Pascal set, but are found in Turbo. Some are also used in other versions of the language.

asm   Marks the start of a block of assembly code, within the Pascal program.

constructor   Used in Turbo's object oriented extensions to the language. Sets up an object containing virtual methods.

destructor   Another object oriented facility, this removes an object from memory.

exports   Used in the creation of DLL code, to make procedures and functions accessible by calling programs.

implementation   When creating free-standing units, this marks the start of the code defining its procedures and functions.

inline   Marks the start of a block of machine code embedded in a program.

interface   When creating *units*, marks the area in which procedures and functions are declared.

library   Marks the start of code to be compiled as a DLL.

object   Used in defining structures in object oriented programming.

shl   **sh**ift **l**eft, multiplies a (binary) number by two.

shr   **sh**ift **r**ight, divides a (binary) number by two.

string   Equivalent to *packed array [1..x] of char.* If followed by a number, strings are fixed length (e.g. string[40]), otherwise of variable length.

unit   Marks the start of code that will be compiled as a unit.

uses   Starts a list of units to be incorporated into a program.

> ## Tip
>
> For more about DLLs and other aspects of Windows programs, try the companion book *Windows Programming Made Simple.*

Procedures

append   Opens a file and moves the file pointer to the end where new data will be written. In standard Pascal the form is:
    assign(filename, 'diskfile');

close   Moves any data in the file buffer to disk and closes the file. (Page 106)

dispose   Returns dynamically allocated memory to the heap. (Page 143)

freemem   As **dispose**, but specifying the size of the memory to be returned.

get   An alternative to **read** for transferring data from disk to memory. Not used in Turbo Pascal.

getmem   As **new**, but with variables of specified size.

new   Creates storage by dynamic memory allocation. (Page 143)

put   An alternative to **write** for transferring data to disk. Not used in Turbo.

randomize   Sets a starting value (from the system clock) for the random number generator. If not used, **random** always produces the same sequence of numbers. (Page 48)

read   Reads a record from disk into a variable, or reads values from the keyboard into variables. (Page 15 and 105)

readln   Performs a **read**, then removes the carriage return. (Page 14)

reset   Opens a file for reading or writing. (Page 104) In standard Pascal the form is:
    reset(filename, 'diskfile');

rewrite   Opens a new file, overwriting any existing file of the same name. (Page 104) In standard Pascal the form is:
    rewrite(filename, 'diskfile');

seek   Moves to a given position on a file. (Page 124)

write   Writes a record to a disk file, or writes data on screen or text file, leaving the cursor at the end of the text. (Pages 5 and 105)

writeln   Performs a write, then moves the cursor to the next line. (Page 5)

Turbo Pascal procedures

Assign   Links a file variable to a disk file. The file can then be opened with **reset**, **rewrite** or **append**. (Page 105)

BlockRead   Reads a block of data from disk into a variable. This block will usually contain one or several records.

BlockWrite Writes a block of data to disk from a variable.

ChDir   Changes the current directory within a program.

Dec   Decrements (reduces by 1) the value in an integer or longint variable.

Delete   Removes a given number of characters from a string. (Page 88)

Erase   Deletes a file on the disk.

Exit   Forces an exits from a loop or other block of code.

FillChar   Fills a given number of bytes of a string with a character; .e.g. **FillChar(uline,40, '-')** fills the string *uline* with dashes.

Flush   Moves any data in the buffer into a text file, useful when printing from within a program.

GetDir   Returns the name of the current directory.

Halt   Forces an immediate end to a program.

Inc   Increments (increases by 1) the value in an integer or longint variable.

Insert   Inserts a substring into a string at a given point. (Page 88)

MkDir   Creates a new directory in the current directory.

Move   Copies a number of bytes from one variable to another. These need not be of the same type.

Rename   Renames a file on the disk.

RmDir   Deletes a directory. This only works if the directory is empty.

RunError   Forces an end to the program and generates an error code. Used in advanced debugging.

ScrollTo   Scrolls the screen window to a location specified by X,Y co-ordinates.

SetTextBuf   Assigns a buffer (block of memory) to a text file. Data is then copied as a block into the buffer, and read from there, rather than directly from disk, speeding up file access.

Str   Converts an integer or longint value to a string. This could then be **concat**'d with other strings, or otherwise manipulated for display.

Truncate   Used with a sequential file, this puts an end of file marker at the current position, abandoning any old data beyond that point.

Val   Converts a number in string form into an integer value – almost the same as the getint function shown on page 98.

Take note

Turbo Pascal for Windows also has a great many other procedures that link to the Windows application program interface.

Functions

abs	Gives the absolute value of number of any type; e.g. abs(-4) = 4.
arctan	The arctangent turns a tangent value into an angle.
chr	Converts an ASCII code number into a character. (Page 79)
cos	The cosine of an angle.
eof	When true, shows that the end-of-file has been reached. (Page 107)
eoln	When true, shows that the end-of-line has been reached in a text file.
exp	The exponential, turns a logarithm into a denary value.
frac	The fractional part of a real number.
int	The integer part of a real number.
ln	The natural logarithm of a real number.
ord	Mainly used for converting a character into an ASCII code, but gives the ordinal number of any value of an ordinal type.
pred	Given a value of any ordinal type, this returns its predecessor (the one before it); e.g. pred(2) = 1; pred('G') = 'F'.
random	Generates a pseudo-random number. (Page 48)
round	Converts a real number to the nearest integer.
sin	The sine of an angle.
sqr	Give the square of any numeric value, with the type matching the input value's type.
sqrt	The square root – works only with real numbers.
succ	Gives the successor (the one after) of any ordinal value.
trunc	Truncates a real-type value to an Integer-type value.

> ## Take note
>
> Arctan, cos and sin work with angles expressed in radians, not degrees. (2 * Pi radians = 360 degrees.)

Turbo Pascal functions

Addr	The memory address of an object pointed to by a pointer.
Concat	Joins two or more strings into one. (Page 88)
Copy	Copies part of a string into another. (Page 88)
CSeg	Used mainly in assembler programming, this tells you the value of the CS (Code Segment) register – i.e. where the program is located in memory.
DSeg	This gives the value of the DS (Data Segment) register – i.e. the start of the storage area for variables.
FilePos	Returns the current position, where the next record will be read or written, in a file.
FileSize	Gives the size, in bytes, of a file.
Hi	Returns the high byte of a two-byte word.
IOResult	Equal to zero if the last I/O operation was successful. Useful for checking that a file exists and can be opened, before trying to read it.
Length	The length of a string. (Page 88)
Lo	Returns the low-byte of a two-byte word.
MaxAvail	Tells you the size of the largest block of free space in heap memory.
MemAvail	Gives the total amount of free space in the heap.
Odd	Tests integer and longint values, returning true if the number is odd.
Ofs	The offset (number of bytes) of a variable's storage space from the start of its segment in memory.
ParamCount	The number of parameters after the program name in the command line used to start it.
ParamStr(n)	Gives the nth command-line parameter.
Pi	The value of Pi, accurate to 10 decimal places (3.1415926536)
Pos	Returns the position of a matching substring within a string, or zero if no match is found. (Page 88)

Ptr	Converts a segment address (from Seg) and an offset (from Ofs) into a pointer value.
SeekEof	The same as **eof**, though only applicable to text files.
SeekEoln	The same as **eoln**, though only applicable to text files.
Seg	The address of the start of the segment containing a specified object.
SizeOf	The size in bytes of a variable – mainly used on records.
SPtr	The value of the SP register; i.e. the address of the Stack Pointer.
SSeg	The value of the SS register; i.e. the address of the Stack segment.
Swap	Swaps the high and low bytes of a two-byte word.
UpCase	Converts a character to upper case.

Index